Acknowledg...

Much thanks to Dan Lundy for his work typing the manuscript. Thanks to Pat Raines for the details of footnoting and other resources used in this book. For their work on the manuscript, thanks to Frank Whitsitt and Diane Samson.

LIVING LIFE TO THE
MAX

Solomon's Wisdom for Christian Living

VERNON ARMITAGE
WITH MARK LITTLETON

BARBOUR
PUBLISHING

LIVING LIFE TO THE
MAX

Solomon's Wisdom for Christian Living

Published in cooperation with Winsun Literary, Gladstone, Missouri.

Published by Barbour Publishing, Inc., P.O. Box 719, Uhrichsville, Ohio 44683
www.barbourbooks.com

Our mission is to publish and distribute inspirational products offering exceptional value and biblical encouragement to the masses.

Member of the
Evangelical Christian
Publishers Association

Printed in the United States of America.
5 4 3 2 1

Dedication

To my wife, Charlene, my greatest encourager

CONTENTS

CHAPTER 1

PUTTING THE
PUZZLE
PIECES
OF LIFE TOGETHER

Introducing the Wisdom of the Proverbs

Wisdom is the most important thing; so get wisdom.
If it costs everything you have, get understanding.

PROVERBS 4:7 NCV

Have you ever wondered how you can make life really work? I find that many lives today are like Humpty Dumpty, teetering on that wall. Every once in awhile, life crashes down, and Humpty Dumpty lies at the bottom of the wall, broken and in despair. All the king's men gather around, but no one knows what to do, and they end up wringing their hands with frustration and crying: "It can't be fixed!"

Of course, Humpty could always trek down to the local counselor's office and fork over $50 to $100 per session to learn that he's broken and he can be fixed—if he returns each week for a year!

I won't charge you that much for the counsel in this book— some of the best counsel you'll ever receive. How do I know that? Because I've taken this counsel and used it in my life. When I fell off that wall I found that not only could I be fixed, but I could also learn and grow through the situation to God's glory.

That's what our lives are all about, isn't it? God's glory?

Anyone who wants to live life for God will soon discover that God wants us to live it to the max. And that's what King Solomon tells us.

So what's the problem?

It's all over the face of the map. Humpty Dumptys everywhere are getting their faces smashed and their lives wrecked.

You've probably heard that somewhere around 50 percent of marriages fail today. That's just one statistic. If people aren't dealing with marriage problems, they may be struggling financially with credit-card debt and bankruptcy. Others work hard to keep together their relationships, jobs, children, and emotions. But often, when we enter the counseling chamber, it seems that no one really knows how to put us together again. We all have areas of our lives that we are trying desperately to hold together but which appear to be ready to blow apart at any moment.

ONE FAMOUS CORNER OF THE WORLD

Hollywood exemplifies the problem. There, we often see that those with the most beauty, wealth, and success cannot manage their own lives. One of my favorite television programs is *Biography* on A&E. I'm saddened to see how many of these celebrities have failed miserably in some area of life. In fact, some of them have become suicidal over their despair at trying to fix some broken area of their lives. On the outside, they are envied by many people. On the inside, though, too often they are simply people who have been unable to put their lives together.

Whenever I sit down with people troubled by problems and situations they've been unable to change, I always turn to the same source: God's Word. In it we find something called "wisdom."

What is wisdom? It's the mental capacity God has for making things work, making lives grow, making people whole. Through wisdom, God created the universe, including you and me. Psalm 139 tells us that He knit us together cell by cell until our bodies became objects of perfection in His eyes. In the process, He also designed our mental abilities, emotions, and spirits into people with a purpose.

What do I mean by "purpose"? Consider a man who builds a small two-person sailboat. He has a purpose in mind for that vessel. Perhaps he imagines sailing it on a bright sunny day on a small lake.

Now imagine the people involved in constructing a giant ocean liner. Its purpose is to travel safely across the ocean, to endure rough weather, waves, and rain, to get a boat full of people and cargo safely to a destination.

What if you mix up the purposes on these two pieces of sailing equipment? If you decide to use that little sailboat to sail across the Pacific Ocean or put the ocean liner in a small lake, both vessels are headed for trouble. Their designs determine where they're used.

Similarly, when we live outside of the design God planned for us, we become either capsized when hit with a hurricane or just plain grounded in the mud, feeling that life has proven too difficult for us to survive.

Through wisdom we begin to grasp God's purpose. Then

we can succeed in life on the basis of the design God gave us. This wisdom that created the universe and all of life is still available to us, too. How?

THE HANDBOOK

You probably know what I'm going to say next. But it's true.

God gave us a handbook—the Bible. Written over a span of sixteen hundred years by more than forty authors on three continents in three languages, the Bible has one consistent story and theme running through it—God loves mankind and sent His Son to redeem it. This alone shows us the unity of purpose that went into writing the Bible. The Bible discusses many subjects from the story of creation to the problems of adultery, abortion, and homelessness.

Imagine bringing together ten authors today from similar backgrounds. Do you think they could write on any single subject with much agreement and consistency? Hardly. But the Bible, with its forty authors, agrees in all parts. Why? Because God's hand guided the writing of our Bible through the centuries. His purpose was that we might know Him and His plan for our lives.

This book focuses on one chapter of God's handbook—Proverbs. Amazingly enough, this timeless volume addresses many issues that people struggle with every day.

THE PROVERB

Proverbs is made up of precisely what its title suggests: proverbs.

What, then, is a proverb?

Cervantes, the Spanish poet, once said a proverb is "a short sentence based on long experience." The dictionary defines it as a short, popular saying expressing obvious truth. So Proverbs is a book filled with concise sayings of practical truth that can guide us in our daily lives. It's God's how-to book for wise living.

Written mostly by Israel's King Solomon, the wisest man on earth (around 900 B.C.), Proverbs is really the message of a father telling his son the right ways to live. In fact, the Book of Proverbs was collected to be used by the young men of Israel's society.[1] These young people, groomed for positions of leadership, would read and memorize its contents so they could grow in wisdom and in the knowledge of God.

Wisdom is the central theme in this book of advice. "Wisdom is the most important thing; so get wisdom. If it costs everything you have, get understanding" (Proverbs 4:7 NCV).

I do a double take when I read a verse like this. It reminds me that wisdom is paramount, and getting it is a prime responsibility for those who would live well, honestly, and successfully.

A good one-word definition for wisdom is "skill"—a God-given skill for using your knowledge. In the Old Testament, the Hebrew word for "wise" *(hakam)* is also used to describe a craftsman who helped build the tabernacle and Solomon's temple.[2]

Knowledge is worth little if you don't have the skill to use it! You might have a college education and not be very smart in the way you live. Dr. Roy Zuck, a writer and teacher at Dallas Theological Seminary, said it well: "Wisdom means being skillful and successful in one's relationships and responsibilities. . .observing and following the Creator's principles of order in the moral universe."[3]

It is not enough to have knowledge. We must have wisdom or the skill to use that knowledge. The pages of history are filled with names of brilliant people who were knowledgeable enough to become rich and famous, but not wise enough to know how to really live.

What is the source of wisdom? The Book of Proverbs informs us that only the Lord gives wisdom (Proverbs 2:6). He gives the knowledge and understanding that build wisdom.

CONNECT WITH GOD

Amazingly, wisdom has very little to do with IQ. Incredibly smart people can be failures in some of the most basic areas of life—relationships, discipline, and character. Conversely, people with low IQs can be amazingly wise. Wisdom doesn't come to us by sitting in a classroom and taking notes from a professor. Rather, it's a skill that God alone can give. So the first step toward gaining wisdom is getting to know God personally.

How do you connect with God like that?

This book is not meant to be an evangelism tool, but I want to ask you to think clearly and hard about your relationship with God. Is He part of your life? Does He speak to you at times? Are you listening? Do you pray? Have you seen answers to your prayers?

If you can say yes to all of these questions, you've probably made a strong connection with God. However, if you're not sure, let me make it easy for you.

The first step to knowing God is entrusting God with your life—your mind, your heart, your soul, and your body.

Look at Proverbs 9:10 (NIV): "The fear of the LORD is the beginning of wisdom, and knowledge of the Holy One is understanding." Bible knowledge starts with a personal relationship with God. Stop and think about this for a moment. If you miss this, nothing else in this book will work for you.

For instance, pretend that I believe I'm the person who makes up all the rules in my life. And I've decided to believe that two plus two is five. Even though many people may try to tell me it's four, I've decided it's five. So, when I go to the supermarket to buy groceries, I end up arguing with the cashiers because they tell me two plus two is four while I, in my blithe belief that I call the shots, believe it's five.

Next, I visit the bank and am soon plunged into even more serious problems. In fact, everywhere I turn, I find nothing in my life fits together because I have violated the basic law that two plus two is four.

Many people violate the basic laws of life by thinking they can live life without God. They'll go their own way or perhaps try another religion. But in time, they find that life doesn't work. They need to connect with the One who is truth.

The most basic spiritual law of wisdom is knowing Jesus Christ as your Savior and Lord. Unless you know Him personally, you'll never find the wisdom and peace of putting life together. It's that simple.

How do you know Jesus as your personal Savior? By trusting Him with your life and everything you are. By opening your heart to Him and asking Him to save you, forgive you for your sins, and become Lord of your life.

It's really that simple. God created a doorway to heaven in Jesus. If we enter that doorway, heaven opens to us and we become God's children.

That is the first necessary step to gaining God's wisdom on any level.

What, then, are other steps you can take to building your life on Christ and His wisdom?

LONG FOR WISDOM

We gain wisdom as the longing for wisdom is a consistent priority in our lives.

Proverbs 2:2 tells us to "tune [our] ears to wisdom, and concentrate on understanding" (NLT). Understanding what? Understanding God! Cry out for insight and understanding; search for it as you would for hidden treasure. Go to God and tell Him how much you want to be wise. Do you think He'd refuse to answer such a prayer? But watch out. If you pray for patience, what's the first thing God will do? Send you into situations that stretch your patience. He'll put you into circumstances where you have to be patient.

The same thing happens with wisdom. If you ask God for wisdom, He will answer by putting you into situations in which you have to learn to use His Word and His Spirit to solve those problems.

I tell people if they want wisdom, go after it with the same intensity they have when they've lost money or something very precious to them.

A number of years ago, my wife, Charlene, and I were

traveling in Oklahoma City. We rose early to get ready to go to church. As we dressed, though, Charlene could not find her wedding ring. Now I don't know about you, but this was a number-one crisis for us! We turned that room upside down. She suggested it might have come off when she was washing her hands. At that point, still dressed for church, I crawled under the sink, took the trap off, and cleaned it out, searching for the ring.

Still, no ring.

We packed our luggage in despair, still searching, and then started for church. That was when Charlene put her hand in her pocket. As Paul Harvey would say, "Now you know the rest of the story."

Thinking of that desperation and frantic searching, I wonder how much wisdom someone would find if they sought it with the same determination and intensity. God says that's the same attitude, though, that we must have in looking for wisdom. When seeking wisdom, give it all that's within you. Give it all of the energy you have!

How do we seek that wisdom? First by studying God's Word—the Bible. You might want to read a psalm or proverb every day, read through one of the Gospels (Matthew, Mark, Luke, or John), or begin in Romans and read through the New Testament. You might try a study guide on a specific book to help you spend thirty minutes a day letting God talk to you through His Word. The Bible says God's Word is "living and active" (Hebrews 4:12 NIV). That means when you study God's Word, you can expect your life to change. The key is to spend a small but consistent time each day reading Scripture. Over time, God will begin to change your life.

When we read the Bible, God talks to us. When we pray, we talk to God. Through the combination of consistent prayer and Bible study, we can get quite a dialogue going with God!

The Bible also instructs us to pray for wisdom and understanding. "But if any of you lacks wisdom, let him ask of God, who gives to all generously and without reproach, and it will be given to him" (James 1:5 NASB). Jesus also said that when we pray according to God's will, He will answer (see Matthew 7:7–8).

Here's a key to finding wisdom: Surround yourself with others who have a similar goal. A fire grows hot when many logs are piled on it. If you remove one stick from the fire, however, it may stay hot for awhile, but eventually it will smolder and go out. That log needs the heat from the other logs to keep burning brightly. Likewise, we need the encouragement of others at a local church to keep our spiritual lights burning brightly.

HAVE RESPECT FOR GOD

A third step for gaining wisdom is to have a deep respect for God and His Word.

Check out Proverbs 9:10 (NIV) again: "The fear of the LORD is the beginning of wisdom, and knowledge of the Holy One is understanding." What does it mean to fear the Lord? It means to greatly respect or deeply reverence the Lord—to give Him the same kind of respect you would give a president, a leader, or a beloved friend.

You do not get wisdom by depending on the great American poll, either. For instance, a pupil brought a pet rabbit to school. The children wanted to name the rabbit, but that raised the question of whether it was a boy or girl. One of the pupils said she knew how to tell—they should vote on it.

That sounds good until you realize it doesn't work. That rabbit is male or female regardless of what the vote says.

In this respect, some people believe that wisdom is simply what most people think. It is not. Just consider how popular opinion has changed our society's ideas about premarital sex or sexual orientation in the last few years. If we got wisdom by voting on it, we might be changing our lifestyles every few minutes!

No, God's wisdom is not the majority's opinion. God alone is the source of real wisdom, and having respect for what God says is right or wrong is the starting place for building wisdom into our lives.

CHOOSE FRIENDS CAREFULLY

Another bit of wisdom from Solomon on how to gain wisdom: Choose your friends carefully.

Proverbs 13:20 (NIV) says, "He who walks with the wise grows wise, but a companion of fools suffers harm." What are the greatest influences of our lives? Parents, friendships, or a close relationship. People who become intimate with us always have the greatest impact.

In fact, even being surrounded by people from another culture can influence us. We all know people who've spent time in the South and return with a bit of a drawl and a mouthful of "y'alls." We can easily pick up idiosyncrasies from others without realizing it. With this in mind, we must choose our friends carefully. You can't hang around with turkeys and expect to fly like an eagle.

Years ago, I looked very different from the way I look now. At one point, I wore my hair fairly long and dressed in shoes that made me two to three inches taller. My friend Bill decided to go for the same look, especially the high-heeled shoes, despite his wife's misgivings. He said, "If Pastor Armitage can wear them, so can I."

After church one Sunday, as I greeted a long line of people, Bill staggered up and promptly fell down the stairs because he wasn't used to the heels. He looked up at me and said, "I don't care if you do wear them. I'm not wearing them anymore."

With that, he tore off the shoes and left them sitting there.

Bill learned that just because his friends do something they like doesn't mean he should do that. And some friends will do things that are far more dangerous than shoes with high heels. Watch out. The devil will work through people close to you if you're not careful.

REBUKE

Here's one last bit of guidance as you seek wisdom: Pay attention to rebuke.

Proverbs 1:23 (NIV) tells us, "If you had responded to my rebuke, I would have poured out my heart to you and made my thoughts known to you."

A rebuke is when you speak the truth, even if it may sting a bit. Receiving a rebuke is one of the most powerful ways to learn and grow. People take a chance when they speak the truth to you. They can't know how you will react. They risk your displeasure and possibly worse. But when you consider the courage it takes for someone to tell you what he or she sees in your life as wrong, you know it comes from a caring, loving heart.

I remember coming home from college one day and seeing my best friend from high school. I had not been in college very long, but I thought I already knew everything. I was spouting off inappropriately about somebody, and my friend Bob looked at me with piercing eyes. He said, "Vernon, you should never talk that way."

That stopped me right in my tracks. I realized he was right. I was gossiping and complaining, two things the Bible condemns. I needed his rebuke right then.

DON'T BE FOOLISH

The Book of Proverbs features another theme we should be aware of: not being a fool.

What is a fool? People who do not act with wisdom are called fools, and their behavior is described as folly or foolishness. Folly is the opposite of wisdom, and a fool is the opposite of a wise person.

What does a fool do?

First, he trusts only in himself. Proverbs 28:26 (NIV) tells us that "he who trusts in himself is a fool, but he who walks in wisdom is kept safe." Proverbs 14:12 (NIV) says, "There is a way that seems right to a man, but in the end it leads to death." How do you know right from wrong? Do you realize you can be sincerely wrong? Without God's wisdom, you may do strange and foolish things.

In 1997, some people near San Diego, California, were involved in the Heaven's Gate cult. Thirty-nine members of the cult committed suicide in March because they thought a UFO following the tail of the Hale Bop comet would transport them to heaven. Members of the group had even looked through a high-powered telescope and returned it to the store saying it didn't work because it didn't show the UFO.

These tragic deaths were the result of people sincerely believing things that were just plain dumb. Foolish!

While the beliefs of the Heaven's Gate cult may seem crazy to us, perhaps to a lesser degree we do foolish things all the time. We foolishly believe no one will learn when we sneak onto Internet pornography. We foolishly believe our office gossip won't get back to the person we slander. We foolishly think excessive credit-card debt won't get us into financial trouble. We foolishly believe we can win at the casino over the long haul and that fat-free ice cream won't make us fat. The list goes on and on. Without God's wisdom in our lives, our behavior will become foolish.

The second thing a fool does is find pleasure in evil. Proverbs 10:23 (NIV) states it well: "A fool finds pleasure in evil conduct, but a man of understanding delights in wisdom."

A theme of the 1960s was, "If it feels good, do it." Living by feelings alone is foolish. When we operate on feelings, we often forget the consequences of some actions. You can't live by what feels right. It may feel good for the moment to cheat on your taxes, to seek revenge, or to have an affair, but we know better. Living by what feels good will bring you to disaster.

Third, a fool acts before he thinks. Proverbs 12:23 (NIV): "A prudent man keeps his knowledge to himself, but the heart of fools blurts out folly."

Do you remember what happened to Peter the night before Jesus was crucified? Jesus told all of the disciples they would fall away. Peter arrogantly said, "Even if all fall away on account of you, I never will" (Matthew 26:31, 33 NIV). Jesus then informed Peter that before the cock crowed he would deny even knowing Jesus three times. Do you remember what Peter did? After he denied the Lord, he went out and wept bitterly. He wasn't thinking before he acted.

Fourth, fools don't listen to advice. Proverbs 15:5 (NIV) tells us, "A fool spurns his father's discipline, but whoever heeds correction shows prudence."

Who in your life right now will be honest enough to tell you when you're wrong? How do you respond when that person tells you of your fault? How well do you listen to honest rebuke? I've heard, "If one man calls you a donkey, pay him no mind, but if two men call you a donkey, get a saddle. They're probably right."

Fifth, a fool doesn't learn from his or her mistakes. I appreciate the graphic words of Proverbs 26:11 (NIV): "As a dog returns to its vomit, so a fool repeats his folly." A fool doesn't learn from his errors.

Two men went on a hunting trip to Alaska. They landed on a lake in a small plane with pontoons, where the pilot left them. When the pilot returned for them, each had killed a moose. After the pilot loaded the hunters and their gear, he realized the plane was at maximum weight. Their catch would have to stay.

"But our pilot last year loaded our moose, and his plane was the same size plane as this one," the men told the pilot.

"Really?" said the pilot. "Well, I guess we can give it a try." With that he strapped a moose on each pontoon.

They sputtered to the end of the lake to get the longest possible takeoff. He shoved the throttle forward. They began to move, and finally, they lifted off the lake, just skimming the treetops. But the pilot was right. The plane was seriously overloaded and crashed minutes into the flight.

Both hunters were knocked unconscious but came to at about the same time. The first hunter looked around at the mess—moose meat and plane parts everywhere. "Where are we?" he asked his partner.

"About fifty yards from where we crashed last year," his partner replied.

As the Proverbs writer said, sometimes we go back like a dog to the same vomit and do it all over again. If you have cycles of foolishness in your life, you can decide to stop. All the king's horses and all the king's men cannot put Humpty Dumpty back together again, but the wisdom of God can.

The principles from Proverbs in the chapters ahead will help us to build the foundation of our lives on a solid rock. Then we can hold our lives together when trouble comes our way.

CHAPTER 2

A CEO's Guide to Good

DECISION

MAKING

The Proverbs' Four-Step Process

The Lord has determined our path;
how then can anyone understand the direction his own life is taking?

PROVERBS 20:24 TEV

That Tuesday came cold and stark. The space shuttle, ready to launch from Cape Canaveral, glistened in the sunlight. What most Americans didn't know was that an argument raged inside the control center. Engineers and technicians argued over whether the Challenger should even be launched that morning, January 28, 1986. Temperatures had dropped too low for the launch to be safe, some said. But the countdown continued. The "go for it" group won.

Liftoff went fine, but seventy seconds later, the Challenger exploded and its crew perished. Nothing was left but the debris that fell out of the sky for a full hour.

The worst had happened because of a bad decision.[1]

God has given us the wonderful ability and freedom to make choices. Decision making is an indispensable part of putting life together. If you flunk at making decisions, you'll flunk much of life. If you do well at making decisions, you'll do well at putting together the pieces of life.

Most problems that enter our lives can be traced to poor decisions. For example, problems with business, marriage, children, priorities, morals, ethics, spiritual issues, time management, stress, health, and money usually relate to bad decisions we've made.

Patrick Morley, a successful businessman, says, "We are each branded by the decisions we make; we are the sum of our decisions. Decision making determines who and what we are more than any other aspect of our lives."[2]

I believe this is true. Chance doesn't lead one to his destiny; choice does.

DIFFERENT KINDS OF DECISIONS

We make decisions on many levels. For example, some decision making is minor. You go to the grocery store and decide to buy potato chips. Have you ever noticed how many different potato chips line the shelves? There are flat chips, ruffled chips, sour cream chips, barbecue chips, fat-free chips, and it goes on and on. Mr. Potato must feel very good about himself. We have dressed him up in many ways. Then at the end of the potato chip line comes what? Corn chips. And then you have all the varieties of Fritos, Doritos, etc. So how do you make those minor decisions? Just get one, or a bag of each of them, or maybe whatever is on sale. It certainly won't be an earth-shaking decision.

Other decisions involve priorities, such as, "Do I do homework, or do I go out with my friends?" What do you put as priority?

Finally, we get to major decisions. One major decision I had to make happened when my dad was sick in the hospital, and I had to decide whether to remove him from life support. I still remember the doctor saying, "I need to talk to you." I listened to the doctor, and being the only child, I had to decide on my own. At the same time, I was also making decisions about my mother's cancer treatment. It was a tough period of decision making, but I believe God led me to do the right thing in each case.

Some decisions are defining moments in our lives. By that I mean you make a decision that will, in many ways, define the outcome of the rest of your life. I had no idea how big a major decision could be when I was deciding which college to attend. I faced many choices, but I chose the college where I later met my wife, Charlene. The decision I made about college resulted in a defining moment in my life. If I had not gone to that college, I might never have met the mother of our children. My life could have gone in a much different direction.

Another important decision was whether or not to attend seminary and which seminary. I had almost decided to go to Southern Seminary in Kentucky, but at the last minute, Charlene and I agreed to at least go to Kansas City and find out what Midwestern Seminary offered. I remember visiting a class taught by Dr. W. B. Coble. After his lecture he said, "You are children of the King, so act like it."

That phrase hit me hard because I'd been thinking about who I was in Christ. I looked at Charlene when Dr. Coble said that, and she turned to me, astonished. We knew at that moment that God wanted us at Midwestern. I would never have even known about the church where I serve, Pleasant Valley, if I had not made this decision. It was a defining moment, leading to consequences that defined the rest of my life.

Still another kind of choice is the moral decision—the choices we make between right and wrong. Sometimes these seem to be innocent decisions, like which TV programs to watch. But the choice of which program to watch can suddenly change from a minor decision to a moral decision.

The two boys who killed so many students at Columbine High School immersed themselves in the media culture, from television to video games. They played the latter for hours, even modifying one game to match the layout and corridors of the high school they intended to attack. I would suspect that drinking in the violence they enjoyed through those fantasy games played a part in leading them to make the terrible decisions that led to the real-life massacre.

And what about the electronic game industry? It is now a multibillion-dollar business, more than twice what we spend at the movie box office! How do parents decide on these little, simple things like video games that have become major and moral decisions?

We still haven't seen the end of the genetic technology boom. We're already confronted by cloning. One day soon we may all have the opportunity to clone ourselves, receiving a human being whom we'd use as a source of new organs, should ours wear out.

You and your family may very well face big moral issues this next decade. How do we make good decisions?

The Information Age

Patrick Morley says, "The best insurance for making the right decision is to know how not to make the wrong decisions. This technical world we live in with high-tech has not helped us. A high-tech world gives us more information and more options, but not wisdom."[3]

John Naisbitt says, "The most dangerous promise of technology is that it will make our children smarter."[4]

However, all of the technology we're inventing today will not make us wiser. Access to information will not teach us how to analyze or put our lives back together. It only throws out more mindbombs that make sorting out life more complicated.

Every year you face many more choices. In fact, they become more numerous every day of our lives. But I have good news for you. The Book of Proverbs gives us relevant help for today in putting our lives together. Let me give you some of the verses in Proverbs that point to four different steps of decision making.

Enter: God

Number One: The first step of good, solid decision making is to look to God.

Proverbs 2:6 (NIV) tells us that "the LORD gives wisdom, and from his mouth come knowledge and understanding." The key to making good decisions is knowing God and exercising your God-given wisdom. Our wisdom will never rise above the level of our understanding of God.

I once read of a study in which people were asked different

questions about God. One young woman who was living with her boyfriend, drinking excessively, abusing drugs, and engaging in other immoral things was asked, "What do you think God thinks about the decisions that you're making and about the way you're living?"

Her comment was, "Well, my God is sort of a grandfatherly type; He loves me and takes care of me and tells me I'm okay. He knows boys will be boys and girls will be girls, and He doesn't really care that much what I do."

That's a distorted view of God and will lead to poor decision making. That view of God can ultimately lead a person to justify any lifestyle.

One of Satan's greatest tactics is to distort how you see God. That's what he did to Adam and Eve. He first distorted what God had said about eating fruit in the Garden of Eden (Genesis 3:1–7). He accused God of saying they couldn't eat any fruit in the Garden. Then he put doubt in Eve's mind about what would really happen if she did eat from the forbidden tree. Guess what happened in their lives? They fell, and the consequences of that sin still reverberate in the world today. All of us are born with the same penchant for evil.

God wants us to use our freedom to make decisions within the framework of His moral character. We need to make every effort to understand His true nature, and then we will find it easier to make decisions in line with His will.

Many times people will look at God's will as one specific thing. For example, it's God's will that I work at this company, or it's God's will that I live at a certain place. I believe that in the biblical context, God's will does not look quite like that. While at times God wants us to move in a specific direction, in general, God gives us freedom to make choices—several of which could easily be His will.

When our church recently built the largest facility our congregation has ever owned, the process was filled with many decisions. Some of those decisions, like the color of a classroom, were almost trivial. Others were monumental. But frequently, we could have gone two, three, or four different ways, and each would have been just as wise as the others. The principle that overrode everything was that we should build the church "to honor God."

That principle guided everything. When we made decisions, we didn't worry as much about which decision was the best but that we honored God in the process.

OUR PURPOSE

In Proverbs 20:24 (TEV) we find the proverb "The Lord has determined our path; how then can anyone understand the direction his own life is taking?" In other words, we need to understand not only God, but also the purpose for our lives. In general, every Christian's purpose is to know God and make Him known to others. In addition, God has gifted every Christian with spiritual gifts they can use to serve others. A few of these gifts God gives include teaching, mercy, service, or administration.

How do you find out what your gifts are? You might try a personality test and a spiritual gift survey. That will give you a good idea of how God has designed you to serve. When you find out what your spiritual gifts are and begin to use them, you soon sense the fulfillment of knowing God is working through you to reach others.

I struggled with these two elements of decision making in my early days. I tried to understand God, and I wanted to understand His purpose for my life. However, I wanted to be everything except what God designed me to be. For awhile, I planned to go into business. When I sensed that He was calling me into ministry, I wanted to be in music ministry or in youth ministry. I wanted to do anything except what God wanted me to do. But God had designed me to be in the ministry I am in now—preaching the Word and equipping saints so they can serve. Wisdom came to me as I began to know God better and then as I learned what He wanted me to do with my life.

ASK FOR HUMILITY

Another component of wisdom from God about decision making is humility. What is humility? Humility is not thinking too highly or lowly of yourself. For example, when Moses killed an Egyptian (Exodus 2), he was thinking too highly of himself—that's pride. He took on God's job of judge and avenger. As a result, he had to leave the country and ended up herding sheep in the desert, far away from the halls of power.

Out on the far side of the desert, God began to speak to him. Remember the scene at the burning bush (Exodus 3)? Five times Moses came up with excuses about why he really shouldn't be the one to lead the people from Egypt. Now Moses was not thinking too highly of himself; he was thinking too lowly of himself. He said something like, "Oh, God, I can't go back there. I cannot speak. I can't lead. Find someone else."

Have you erred either on one side by being too prideful or on the other by having low self-esteem? To make good decisions, we need to have the appropriate attitude about ourselves. That is humility. Like Moses, even if we don't feel confident, when we focus on an almighty, all-loving God who says we can do something, we can have a right understanding of who we are. Pride says, "I can do it by myself." Poor self-esteem says, "I can do nothing at all." Right humility before God says, "I can do everything through him who gives me strength" (Philippians 4:13 NIV). When I begin to put these three components together—understanding God, knowing His purpose for me, and seeing myself rightly, with humility—I begin to gain the wisdom from God to make right and good decisions.

STUDY THE OPTIONS

A second step to being able to make good solid decisions is learning to look at all of the possible options.

Proverbs 19:2 (NCV) says, "Enthusiasm without knowledge is not good." In other words, do your homework. When you're getting ready to make a decision, get all of the facts you possibly can.

My dad drilled this into me. I drive people crazy when I buy anything major. I go crazy researching all the options. What is worse, I sometimes end up in "analysis paralysis." Sometimes I need to listen to Nike and "Just do it!" So although you can go overboard, doing research can help you make solid, informed decisions.

The next part of this verse says, "If you act too quickly, you might make a mistake." Good decision making involves thinking through the possible consequences of your decision. Young people are notorious for acting too quickly. One day when I was in high school, we were dismissed from school early, and some of the kids decided to go to Forsyth, Missouri, which was a ways from our hometown. They wanted me to go along. I didn't ask where they were going, what they were going to do, or when we'd get back. That was immaterial. The most important thing to me, as a high school student, was to go with my friends and not be left out.

I had a great time until I looked at my watch and realized it was time for me to be home. Then I discovered my friends wanted to go to a movie. I would be very late getting home, and I knew what my dad would say about that!

My folks did not have a phone, so I couldn't call them. And I couldn't muster up the courage to say, "Please take me home."

I don't remember what the movie was. I just know that was the most miserable time I ever spent in my life. I got home that night, and no one was in my house. My parents had gone out frantically searching for me, afraid something terrible had happened. I went to bed, and sometime later I heard them come home. My mother came in and hugged me. I could tell she had been crying. Dad didn't say a thing. They knew I had been through punishment enough already, and they never said anymore about it.

I have to say, though, what that verse says, "If you act too quickly, you might make a mistake," is an understatement! When you get ready to make a decision, get the facts!

GET GOOD ADVICE

The third step in making good, solid decisions is to look to others for advice. Proverbs 1:5 (NIV) says, "Let the wise listen and add to their learning, and let the discerning get guidance."

A wise person will seek out wise counsel. Proverbs 13:10 (NIV) says, "Wisdom is found in those who take advice." Proverbs 12:15 (NIV) adds, "The way of a fool seems right to him, but a wise man listens to advice." Fools have already made up their minds; they're not open to advice.

Are you open to the counsel of others? Students, are you willing to listen to your parents? Parents, are you open to learning something from your children? I can tell if people are open to advice by their inquisitiveness. They ask a lot of questions—and the right questions. Socrates was not wise because he knew all the right answers but because he knew all the right questions to ask.

A number of years ago, I hosted Dr. Robert Schuller for a day. He came to Kansas City for a conference, and I picked him up at the airport and took care of him through the day. I looked forward to it because I wanted to get acquainted with him and to ask him many questions. I wanted to learn.

I had a friend along, and Dr. Schuller sat in the backseat. But instead of us asking him questions, he popped up on the edge of his seat with his head between us and began firing his own questions at us. One after another, after another, after another. I couldn't get my questions in because he was so inquisitive. He wanted to learn about Kansas City, the people he would speak to, what was going on in our church, and on and on.

More recently, I had the privilege of sitting down with Bill Hybels, pastor of Willow Creek Community Church near Chicago. It is the largest church in America and one of the largest churches in the world. It seemed like a great opportunity to ask questions, but guess what? He began to pop questions and take notes. He got his pencil and paper out, and I thought, *What is going on here? I pastor a little church in Kansas City, and a guy who pastors the largest church in the country is asking* me *questions?*

That told me a lot about him. He wanted to learn. He was the mentor, but he was asking the questions. I've found over and over that wise people are open to advice, and they want to learn everything they can.

Whom do you turn to for advice? Does someone give you financial advice? Where do you go for legal advice? Who can help when you need emotional support? I've needed emotional counsel at times in my life. It's humbling to say that you feel like life is falling apart, but at those times you need counseling. I know how difficult it is to seek help. But sometimes you need it. Whom do you turn to? Do you just suck it up and act like you're not depressed? Do you try to act like you don't have bad feelings? All of us have some emotional difficulties somewhere along the way. Where do you turn for help?

In the early 1980s, I nearly put myself out of the ministry because of all of the stress I faced. The church grew over 16 percent in one year, and I worked hard, but at one point I became so depressed I didn't think I could continue. I didn't know what was wrong, why this happened to me.

I finally turned to the best counsel I could find, a psychiatrist who became a good friend. He put me on some medication and we talked through many of my stress points. I eventually came out of it and returned to my normal work, a better and healthier person. Without that advice and help, though, I am certain I would not have survived.

Everyone needs good counselors. Whom do you turn to when some area of your life has gone topsy-turvy?

LOOK AHEAD

The fourth step to making good, solid decisions is found in Proverbs 14:8 (TLB): "The wise man looks ahead. The fool attempts to fool himself and won't face facts."

A wise man thinks about where a decision will lead and what the consequences will be. King David was a great decision maker. He made a tremendous decision to fight Goliath. He made a fine decision when he became close friends with Jonathan. When he went to battle against the Philistines, the Bible says that David asked, "God, should I fight the Philistines or not?"

David made wise decisions because he sought God. When King Saul was trying to kill David, Saul did not know David was hiding in the corner of a cave one day (1 Samuel 24). Saul went into the cave to relieve himself. David's men said, "Now is your chance to wipe the guy out; kill him; he's after you!"

What did David do? He respected the office of the king, and he made the excellent decision to go against the advice of his men. Instead, he took his knife and cut off part of Saul's garment so that Saul would know he could have taken his life.

David made other decisions in his life that weren't so wise.

He decided not to go to battle with his men. While he was at home, he walked out on the balcony and saw Bathsheba bathing on the roof of her house (2 Samuel 11). He asked her to come to his room. You know what happened—David's life from that point was all downhill.

You can make a long string of great decisions, but it's still possible to make a wrong decision that will devastate your life. The integrity one builds over many years can be destroyed in a matter of seconds. We have to think ahead. We have to look down the road and see what consequences may result. Or we may end up destroying every good thing we've ever done.

Planning is part of this, too. Proverbs 21:5 (NIV) tells us, "The plans of the diligent lead to profit as surely as haste leads to poverty." Planning is an important element in decision making, and some decisions need to be made before other decisions.

For instance, if you're single, whom you marry should involve advance decisions. You need to consider not only how attracted you are to someone, but what his or her fundamental belief system is. Paul instructs us to not be unequally yoked with an unbeliever (see 2 Corinthians 6:14). No matter how great the initial infatuation, if you end up in a marriage with someone who makes his or her decisions without considering God, you are headed for trouble. Add children to the mix, and you will face even more difficulties.

The advance decision you can make is to date only Christians. That way you won't fall in love with someone whose life runs in a different direction. Then you won't be unequally yoked with a nonbeliever.

DEAL WITH BAD DECISIONS

What do you do with bad decisions? You will make them. So what do you do when you've blown it? Proverbs 16:1 (TLB) says, "We can make our plans, but the final outcome is in God's hands."

The big difference between King Saul and King David was that David was a man after God's own heart (see 1 Samuel 13:14). The difference showed in the way they handled bad decisions. King Saul made a bad decision while waiting for Samuel to arrive to make a sacrifice (1 Samuel 13). God had forbidden anyone but the prophet from making the offering, but when the prophet did not come on time, Saul decided to make the sacrifice himself. Then when the prophet confronted him, he wouldn't confess that he'd done wrong. He made all kinds of excuses and did exactly what it says in Proverbs: He tried to prove he was right. He wouldn't own up to a bad decision, and God took his kingdom away.

How did David handle a bad decision? When Nathan told David he was guilty of adultery with Bathsheba and the murder of her husband (2 Samuel 12), in effect, David said, "I'm the man, and I'm guilty," and immediately confessed. What a difference!

The first step in dealing with a wrong decision is admitting it and repenting. This means changing the way you think and act. Tell God you were wrong and that you want to change and start living a different way.

We all have scars from bad decisions. You can't get rid of the scars, but God can turn our scars into stars, as one preacher says, that will shine brightly in our lives. It's because of His amazing grace. Through grace, God can make any bad decision turn out for good.

Ultimately, no matter what kind of decision we must make—minor, major, or moral—God can lead us on the right path when we choose to look to Him first, collect facts, seek godly wisdom, and think ahead about where this decision will lead. God is always faithful to answer us and guide us when we seek Him with all of our hearts.

CHAPTER 3

SEX
FOR THE MODERN COUPLE

Following God's Simple Rules

For the lips of an adulteress drip honey,
and her speech is smoother than oil.

PROVERBS 5:3 NIV

Our view of sexuality has changed dramatically during the last four decades. It reminds me of the familiar story of the frog in the kettle of water. Placed into a kettle of hot water, a frog will jump out immediately. It's a cold-blooded creature, and the heat scorches its skin. However, if you place the same frog in a kettle of lukewarm water, he will sit contentedly, not noticing any slight increases in temperature. Eventually, even if you raise the temperature to boiling, the frog won't leap out but will soon be cooked—unaware its environment has changed to a deadly end.

Today, our moral values regarding sexual behavior compare to the frog in the kettle. Our moral underpinning has boiled away and died. We would have leapt out of the kettle in an uproar three or four decades ago if today's morals were thrust upon us. But soaking in the gradually changing moral environment has made us, like the frog, unaware that everything has heated up.

For fifteen hundred years people in Western culture embraced common conceptions about sexuality. Sex was for marriage. Marriage was permanent. Children were the blessing of marriage. And growing old together was regarded as a blessing of God. The only major change made in those years occurred when parents stopped the practice of arranging marriages for their children.

These cultural norms certainly were not flawless. For example, during many of those years, people thought of sex only as something dirty, a part of sinful or lower nature. At other times, a double standard existed that winked at the men if they broke the rules but ostracized the women if they did.

THE SEXUAL REVOLUTION

The modern sexual revolution began in the 1950s and 1960s. I see five major contributors to this revolution.

1. There was penicillin, which curbed the life-threatening sexually transmitted diseases that once kept people from straying into adultery, homosexuality, fornication, and other dangerous sexual practices. People began to believe they had much more sexual freedom.
2. The "pill"—birth control drugs—all but eliminated the risk of pregnancy. Although interestingly, researchers find that despite this supposedly risk-reducing factor, there are many more unwanted pregnancies today than ever before.

3. The "free love" philosophy told us that sex is simply an act of pleasure. Society told us focusing on sex would give us greater individual and psychological freedom.

4. So-called "family planning" organizations grew in power. Some convinced many Americans that teenage sexual activity was inevitable and that the most sensible course of action was to freely dispense contraceptives and abortions. They taught us that an unwanted, unborn baby was nothing more than a lump of tissue that could be removed like a tonsillectomy.

5. Almost all of us have the fifth and most convincing component sitting in our living rooms. Television in the last two decades, probably more than anything else, has influenced our behavior and morality by promoting free sex. Few programs today tout abstinence, the sanctity of marriage, or any other long-held beliefs. Many programs show true love as hopping into the sack on the first date.

A *USA Today* cover-page article says it all: "Today is a different world."[1] The reporters watched prime-time television from April 24 through April 30, 1994, almost a decade ago. In this one-week study, 9 percent—only four sitcoms—showed married sex on the programs as desirable and right. Thirteen sitcoms included unmarried sex; nine showed sex between cheating spouses.

This trend has increased in the last decade. You've flipped

through the channels. You know it's rare to find a fulfilling love relationship or sexual experience between two married people. Television and movies usually don't show sexual relationships within marriage. If sex sells products, it also sells moral values. We've bought into the philosophy completely.

Putting life together successfully requires an understanding of our sexuality. Richard Foster, the Quaker theologian, says, "One of the real tragedies in Christian history has been the divorce of sexuality from spirituality."[2] God has always told us not to separate our sexuality from our spirituality. To misuse or abuse our sexuality is to throw away a vital piece of the puzzle of life for putting it together.

Proverbs is packed with golden nuggets of truth and wisdom regarding our sexuality. The initial intent of the Book of Proverbs was to help raise a crop of young people who might become great leaders. Solomon knew sexuality was an indispensable part of teaching young people how to successfully approach life.

It is no different today. We have a tremendous responsibility to go against the current of the tide to raise a group of young people who understand their sexuality as God has created it. Let's look at seven golden nuggets of wisdom and truth we find primarily in Proverbs 5–6.

MANAGE THE DRIVE

Golden Nugget Number One: We must effectively manage the God-given drive for sex. Proverbs 5:3 (NIV) says, "For the lips of an adulteress drip honey, and her speech is smoother than oil." The author had a way with words, didn't he? He said, "Son, there is an extremely powerful appeal in sex, and you should clearly guard against mismanaging this area."

Sex has tremendous appeal to everyone, and that's the reason marketers use sex to sell products. How many car commercials have pictured a beautiful young woman in the passenger seat? What cigarette commercials don't depict lively, comely women smoking the product around handsome, seductive men?

Why should we so closely guard this drive for the pleasure of sex? Why does God give us this wonderful gift of sex and then restrict it?

We must understand that almost everything in life that possesses great power for good must be restricted. For example, when you awaken from surgery, drugs under the restrictions of a doctor are good and ease the pain. But drugs without restrictions take lives every day in America. Fire is terrific when you sit in front of a crackling fireplace on a cold day, but when not restricted it will burn your house down. Even common things, like water in your house, are wonderful but only when it stays in the proper place. Waking up at two in the morning and hearing water running and finding the toilet overflowing onto the bathroom floor and down into your office is not so wonderful. Life is filled with great things, but most of them need restrictions.

Richard Foster adds, "Sex is like a great river that is rich and deep and good as long as it stays within its proper channel. The moment a river overflows its banks, it becomes destructive, and the moment sex overflows its God-given banks, it too becomes destructive. Our task is to define as clearly as possible the boundaries placed upon our sexuality and to do all within our power to direct our sexual responses into that deep, rich current."[3]

Defining sexuality as only physical diminishes its real meaning. Divorcing sexuality from spirituality makes it not much more than an animalistic act.

Proverbs 5:4–5 (NIV) clearly show us the results of mismanaged sex. Continuing his words about the loose woman, Solomon says, "But in the end she is bitter as gall, sharp as a double-edged sword. Her feet go down to death."

Can you picture a father telling this to his son? "Son, her feet go down to death; her feet lead straight to the grave." He's talking to this young man, and he says, "If you get outside the bank of God's restrictions, you're doomed. You will die."

But what dies?

For one thing, illicit sex brings a physical threat. One night on a talk show a guest mentioned a movie star who had stepped out on his wife and spent a night in a hotel with another woman. The next morning when he woke up, she was gone. He walked into the bathroom and found these words written on the mirror with lipstick, "Welcome to the wonderful world of AIDS."[4]

HIV/AIDS isn't the only physical risk. Recent studies report that approximately 65 million people in the United States are affected by sexually transmitted diseases (STDs) with an additional 15 million acquiring STDs each year. Twenty percent of these victims are under twenty years old. Some of these diseases are deadly, cause infertility, and can't be prevented by condom use.

Not counting HIV/AIDS infections, the number of teenagers and adults infected with these STDs is staggering. For example, a study published in the *New England Journal of Medicine* estimated that 20 percent of all Americans age twelve and over are infected with genital herpes. A three-year study of sexually active female students at a major university found that 60 percent were, at some point, infected with human papillo-mavirus (HPV). This virus causes 98 percent of cancer of the cervix and cannot be prevented by condom use.

What am I saying? Foremost of all—the safe sex message is simply not true. Using a condom does not prevent most STDs. It's just a myth. The only true safe sex is sex God's way—sex that stays within the banks of marriage.

A second threat is emotional. Television sitcoms make us laugh as their players break all the rules, but the scripts never include the weeping and emptiness that remain. What will die if you jump out of the banks God has designed for sex? The emotional life of your marriage will die, for one. Distrust, sus-picion, and jealousy enter. In addition, if you engage in sex before marriage, you're more likely to have difficulties compar-ing your spouse to former partners, as well as facing other emotional and physical issues.

Spiritual death is a third threat. The apostle Paul says in 1 Corinthians 6:18 (NLT), "No other sin so clearly affects the body as this one does." Paul says sexual sin is different from all other sins. Sexual immorality is a sin against your own body. Why is that? Because it affects every part of you, not just the physical body, but also your emotions and spirit. No other sin will influence and affect our lives more. God has designed sex to be a powerful motivator for love, marriage, procreation, and pleasure—and it can be used for good or bad. Nothing is more destructive to our spiritual lives than the sin of jumping out of the banks God has given us for sexual conduct.

ESTABLISH HEDGES

Golden Nugget Number Two: Establish protective hedges around yourself. In Proverbs 7, Solomon says to never forget what he's about to say—run from the seductive woman, don't go near her house, build walls of protection around your home, and don't allow yourself to be vulnerable. Turn away from sexual sin, and flee from youthful lust.

Interestingly, when dealing with Satan, the Scriptures tell us to stand up and resist him, and he'll flee. But what does the Bible say about sexual temptation? Run! Flee! Get out of there! Clearly, you can stand and resist Satan, but when it's a sexual temptation, you are to turn and run with all your might because it can so easily catch and destroy you.

I think of a young couple dating who are so tempted to get involved sexually. They decide the next time they're tempted, they will pray together. This sounds very noble, pious, and spiritual—but it's not following the advice of the Scriptures. The Bible says to run!

Loitering around sexual temptation is like sticking your head into a lion's mouth and praying he doesn't bite you. When you deal with a lion, you run. The same is true for sexual temptation. For this couple, running from sexual temptation might mean avoiding situations in which they are alone and set up to fail.

Jerry Jenkins, author of *Hedges: Loving Your Marriage Enough to Protect It,* has given some very good advice on this subject, especially for men. He offers six ways to protect marriage and to be wise by preparing in advance to resist temptation. This applies to you whether you're married or single.

1. "Whenever I need to meet or travel or dine with an unrelated woman, I make it a threesome. Should an unavoidable, last-minute complication make this impossible, my wife hears it from me first."

2. "I am careful about touching. While I might shake hands or squeeze an arm or shoulder in greeting, I embrace only dear friends or relatives, and only in front of others."

3. "If I pay a compliment, it is on clothes or hairstyle, not on the person herself. Commenting on a pretty outfit is much different, in my opinion, than telling a woman that she herself looks pretty."

4. "I avoid flirtation or suggestive conversation, even in jest." Just don't flirt.

5. "I remind my wife often—in writing and orally—that I remember my wedding vows."

6. "From the time I get home from work until the children go to bed, I do no writing or office work. This gives me lots of time for my family and for my wife and me to continue to court and date."[5]

These may not be your hedges, but what are you doing to protect yourself from sexual temptation?

One way to take a little responsibility for this area is to draft a list, take it to your spouse, and say, "Here are some things I will do to protect myself from being vulnerable." If you're single, show your closest friend the list of specific things you've decided not to do. Ask him or her to keep you accountable to those things. If this is a good friend, he or she will be glad to help out in any way he can. The important thing is to take steps to prevent yourself from getting into trouble. The results of not guarding your life are devastating.

In fact, it could go as far as public disgrace. Look at Proverbs 5:9–11 (TLB): "Lest you fall to her temptation and lose your honor, and give the remainder of your life to the cruel and merciless; lest strangers obtain your wealth, and you become a slave of foreigners. Lest afterwards you groan in anguish and in shame, when syphilis consumes your body."

In high school many of us guys were taught to brag about breaking the rules in the area of sex. I learned later in life that most of those young men who were laughing and bragging often lived lives of emptiness, heartache, and regret.

BE LOYAL

Golden Nugget Number Three: Determine to be loyal. Proverbs 5:15 tells us to drink water from our own wells, or share our love only with our wives. Solomon was very graphic and specific in the way he wrote these pieces of wisdom. Here, he meant the sexual experience is like precious water from your own private well. Don't waste it or spill it in places that will use it up and possibly destroy you in the process. The writer indicates that getting thirsty is natural, just like the meaningful sexual relationship is a natural desire, but remain loyal and find satisfaction in your own well.

How do you develop this kind of loyalty? By just reflecting

on it a moment. Just stop and think about the results of throwing valuable water to someone else's field. We see some of those distressing results in Proverbs 9:17 (NCV). Here, Solomon says, "Stolen water is sweeter, and food eaten in secret tastes better." He's making an honest point. Jumping outside the banks of God's plan for our sexuality and stealing from someone else fascinates and allures us. It looks so good. But in verse 18 Solomon adds that "these people don't know that everyone who goes there dies!"

So before you get into a tempting situation, stop and think about the consequences of such an action. What would this do to your marriage? To your children? To your relationship with God?

And then run away from it for all you're worth.

DEVELOP INTIMACY

Golden Nugget Number Four: Develop intimacy in your relationship with your spouse. Proverbs 5:18–19 (NCV) says you should "Be happy with the wife you married when you were young. She gives you joy, as your fountain gives you water. She is as lovely and graceful as a deer. Let her love always make you happy; let her love always hold you captive." I like that last phrase, "let her love always hold you captive."

Sometimes the greatest defense is a great offense. We've looked at several defensive measures about sexuality. But here Solomon teaches us about offense and how to win the game. You can't win the game just by playing good defense. If you play great football teams and hold them to just one field goal, that's great defense. But you won't win unless you get the ball across the end zone yourself. That's offense.

A great offense against sexual temptation is having fulfilling intimacy in your marriage relationship. Let your wife's love always hold you captive, and let her love consistently draw you back to her.

How do you keep a captivating, intimate love growing? Let me give you three Rs to remember. Essentially, in all of the weddings I preside over, I mention at least two of these words.

Reaffirm. Every single day, in some way, reaffirm your love for one another. The great enemy of intimacy is routine. You're so proud of a new car. You love spending time in the car so much that you'll dream up new reasons just to drive to the store. You make sure no one gets into the new car with dirty feet. The kids don't get in without showering, and you might slip out at noon to wash off a little bit of dirt because it's so precious when it's new. But after awhile the kids can get in dirty, soda gets spilled on it, the muddy dog is even allowed in, and you drive down the highway without even thinking about it. Routine has hardened your heart to that beautiful car.

This isn't much of a problem with a car, but if you do this to a spouse, you're in trouble. Figure out ways to reaffirm your love with words, attitude, gifts, and services like grocery shopping. If you try, you can find all kinds of ways. Be creative.

Dr. Gary Chapman's books on the love languages people communicate in have influenced me very much. My love language tends to be acts of service, while my wife's is words. Thus, on special occasions of the year like Valentine's Day, the most meaningful thing to reaffirm my love for her is what I call a "bouquet of words." I did this one year with the word "Valentine" and made a list of the things I most appreciate about her. My wife always saves these things and cherishes them.

Respect. Respect each other always. When you are first married, you respect how your spouse feels. You wouldn't hurt him or her. You listen attentively to the other's opinion and needs. However, before long routine causes us to lose respect. When respect falters, so does intimacy, because lack of respect always hurts.

I learned respect from my dad. As I watched him value and respect my mother, I was greatly impacted. If they disagreed, they never openly argued before me. I witnessed that respect, and it made me want to practice the same thing in my marriage.

Resolve. You will enjoy very little intimacy in your life without the ability to resolve conflict. Conflict is neither good nor bad; it just is. How you resolve conflict greatly determines the rest of the relationship. You will have conflicts, but resolve them adequately to keep the intimacy growing.

Because I never saw my parents in conflict, when I got married I tended to think we should never have conflict. I would avoid it. I had to learn that conflict is not good or bad. What matters is how you deal with it. When there's a conflict, don't act like there's not conflict, but deal with it.

ESTABLISH CONVICTIONS

Golden Nugget Number Five: Establish deep convictions about sex. Proverbs 6:20 (NIV) says, "My son, keep your father's commands and do not forsake your mother's teaching." This tells me Mom and Dad have a tremendous responsibility to teach. Who has been instructing your child about sexuality? The greatest manual for teaching your child about sexuality is the Book of Proverbs. If you have an adolescent child, for example, assign him or her to read Proverbs 5–7. Then discuss it with your child and begin to teach biblical principles concerning sexuality. Your kids need to understand that they can't wait until they're involved in a relationship to set the rules. You can't start making the rules while you're on a date because then it's too late. You have to set the rules far in advance.

Last year, at the close of one of our church services, many of our students came forward with a card they had filled out. With these cards, they publicly committed to wait until marriage to have sex. Later this year, those cards, along with those from students all over America, were placed on the Golden Gate Bridge. Now kids all over America have put a sign in their yard that says, "True Love Waits." This is establishing convictions in advance. This is something we parents need to stress for our kids before they get out in the tough world of dating.

DEAL WITH LUST

Golden Nugget Number Six: Know how to deal with lust. Proverbs 6:25 (NIV) says, "Do not lust in your heart after her beauty or let her captivate you with her eyes." For you, it may not even be the eyes that are so captivating, but the point is, don't lust after the loose woman. She may be beautiful; she may make eyes at you, but you need to know what she's serving is only lust.

What is lust? Lust is a desire for something forbidden. Lust is a mental activity. No one knows when you're lusting except two people—you and God. Neither your spouse nor your closest friend knows. You can lust at church, at home, in front of the television, or at work, and no one knows it, except for God.

How do you deal with lust, keeping in mind that nearly all sexual mismanagement starts with a mental activity?

Many years ago, author and speaker Josh McDowell led a crusade trying to instruct young people how to understand and deal with their sexuality. As he led lectures across the nation in high schools, he would ask, "What's the greatest sex organ you have?"

The students would become very quiet, wondering where he was going with that. Then he said, "Your brain. This is where it all starts, with the way you think."

That's the reason the apostle Paul said in Romans 13:14 (NIV), "Do not think about how to gratify the desires of the sinful nature." Don't go there! When the thought enters, replace it with another thought! Refuse to let any lust control your life!

GOD IS WATCHING

Golden Nugget Number Seven: Remember, God is always looking. I can see Solomon telling his son, "A man's life is in full view of the Lord. I might not always be there to see all you do, and I might not see what's going through your mind, but God sees and knows everything!" Being aware of God's presence helps us to stay within the banks of His beautiful flowing river of our sexual lives.

When you're tempted to run outside the banks of God's restrictions, just imagine your spouse standing beside you with a baseball bat in his or her hands. That is a powerful picture!

Now I'd like to ask you something very personal. Are you morally pure? You might have blown it pretty big in life. You might be sitting right now on a situation that threatens your very marriage. What do you do? Maybe you haven't done anything with a real person. You're just on the Internet looking at pornographic images. It's currently just a mental stage.

I think King David, more than anyone else, would understand this because of his sin with Bathsheba. What did King David do first in that relationship? He saw her from his roof. He looked, and he lusted. Then he committed adultery. When Bathsheba got pregnant, he committed murder trying to cover up his sin.

What am I trying to say? If you make one mistake and become pregnant, don't make a second mistake by murder or something else. What did David do in the end that helped him get back into the free-flowing river within God's banks? You'll find this guide in Psalm 51.

1. Ask God for mercy. Say, "God, I need your help." Psalm 51:1 (NIV) says, "Have mercy on me, O God."

2. Admit you've sinned. Don't rationalize and say, "I looked at all that stuff on the Internet, but so what? Everybody does." "I watched the TV sitcoms and laughed, so what?" You must reach a place where you admit it's a sin. Verse 4 says, "Against you, you only, have I sinned."

3. Acknowledge God's power to cleanse. Verse 7 says, "Cleanse me with hyssop, and I will be clean;

wash me, and I will be whiter than snow." This is
like a brush dipped in the blood of Christ.

4. Accept God's forgiveness. Verse 13 says, "Then I
    will teach transgressors your ways." I'll change the
    way I'm living and do some positive things by
    serving You. I'm going to run away from this sin.

What about the consequences of sexual sin? Did Bathsheba
become unpregnant when King David did all these things? No.
Did it keep the baby from dying? No, the baby did die. These
actions may not take away the scars or the brokenness in your
life that results from your sin. But if you'll come clean in God's
eyes, He will show you that He is a master at putting together
broken pieces. In fact, in David's life, God demonstrated His
desire to forgive and restore by blessing David and Bathsheba
with a son, Solomon, who would become the next king of
Israel, the wisest man in the world, writer of Proverbs, and an
ancestor of the Messiah, Jesus.

It's well worth following God's simple rules about your
sexuality. It's a wonderful gift. Use it rightly, and you will be
greatly blessed all your days.

CHAPTER 4

RELATIONSHIPS
THAT WILL MAKE
YOUR HEART SING

The Proverbs on People Skills

Spend time with the wise and you will become wise,
but the friends of fools will suffer.

PROVERBS 13:20 NCV

What brings you the greatest joy in life? List three things that come quickly to your mind. These top three will probably have something to do with a relationship.

Isn't this true? The greatest joys in life come from our relationships. People's love, friendship, and help make life meaningful and fulfilling.

Let me ask another question. What gives you the greatest pain in life? Your answer will probably include the same three you just listed. Ironically, relationships bring us great joy but can also bring us great pain. What is the greatest punishment we can give to anyone, excluding capital punishment? Solitary confinement. Many prisoners have cracked under the pressure of solitary confinement. They just couldn't stand being all alone for all those hours of the day.

Have you ever been to Alcatraz as an inmate? Several years ago an ex-inmate of Alcatraz attended our church. He sang in the choir, and he told me some things about this prison that made me want to go and see where he had been. So my son and I visited the prison. The guides took us to the cells that were used for solitary confinement. When the doors closed behind us, it was completely dark. I realized then how terrible this punishment was. Life becomes hellish when all relationships are removed.

A GUIDE TO RELATIONSHIPS

Sometimes people can be very successful in worldly pursuits—job, career, leadership—but fail in developing relationships. Stanford and Harvard Universities and the Carnegie Foundation recently spent one million dollars in a five-year study about job satisfaction and why people stay in or leave a job. They found technical skill was only 15 percent of the reason people get a job, keep a job, and become successful at the job. Eighty-five percent of success on the job has to do with getting along with others—people skills.[1]

How many high schools and colleges offer courses in developing people skills? I'm not aware of any. Isn't that interesting? Eighty-five percent of the reason we can get along, move ahead on the job, and communicate with our spouses and kids doesn't come from technical skills, but from our ability to relate to others.

Though we may not find the help we need in schools, I am grateful we are not left without a guide for handling relationships. Our manual is the Book of Proverbs. Before plunging into what it says about this area, let me point out that if we want to relate well with others, we must first be able to relate well with ourselves.

Look at what Gary Inrig says: "Until we can resolve the fundamental issue of self-worth, we will be crippled for effective relationships."[2] If you can't get along with yourself, who can? If you don't think well of yourself, it will be difficult for others to think well of you.

I have seen this in a positive way with Paul Swadley, my "father" in the ministry. When I was a teenager, he was my pastor. He had a personality like a magnet that drew people to him. He often talked about "liking yourself." That was a new concept to me, and I thought it was a little egotistical, but as I saw him apply it, I realized it was an important quality. It helped me learn to like myself and become more comfortable with relationships.

Let's talk about some of the skills Proverbs offers to us in developing relationships with fellow employees, spouses, parents, friends, and neighbors.

DEVELOP RELATIONSHIPS WITH THOSE WHO ARE WISE

Proverbs 13:20 (NCV) says, "Spend time with the wise and you will become wise, but the friends of fools will suffer." People who become intimate friends greatly impact our lives.

Usually, friends can have a positive influence. We have seen people decide to follow Christ after a friend first built a relationship with them and then talked with them about what it means to know Christ. Someone got close enough to impact them, and now their whole lives have been changed.

Many times our convictions are formed by those who are close to us. These people impact our morals, goals, habits, and the way we talk. Even after years of living in the Kansas City metropolitan area, I still have a southern Missouri accent. I'm branded with this for life. No one ever sat me down and said, "Vernon, we want to teach you to butcher up the English language and sound like someone from the hills." I just hung around southern Missourians so long that I can't get rid of it.

Look again at Proverbs 13:20 (NCV): "Spend time with the wise and you will become wise, but the friends of fools will suffer." King Solomon was considered to be the wisest man in the entire world. But the Bible says his kingdom was eventually stripped from him. Why? Because, according to 1 Kings 11, Solomon married foreign women who did not believe in or love the God of Israel. Their influence pushed his heart away from God to the point that God tore the kingdom in half when Solomon's son Rehoboam came to power. It started because Solomon chose to become intimate with people who drew his heart away from God.

I don't mean we shouldn't have friendships with non-believers. Of course, we should develop meaningful relationships with those outside of the church so they might come to know the Lord. But our primary source of relationship support should come from those who are wise believers in Christ, who are committed to the Bible and God's truth.

BUILD ON SOLID LOYALTY

Proverbs 17:17 (NCV) says, "A friend loves you all the time, and a brother helps in time of trouble." Proverbs 18:24 (NCV) tells us, "Some friends may ruin you, but a real friend will be more loyal than a brother."

You've probably heard that a dog is man's best friend. You can say all kinds of ugly things to your dog and even kick him, but minutes later, he comes to you wagging his tail, convinced you are the supreme ruler of his universe.

You don't always find such commitment among humans, but that kind of loyalty can occur in your relationships. Here's one example:

As a Royal Air Force pilot during World War 2, Peter Foster experienced tremendous adulation and love from the masses. When such pilots walked the streets of London, other people treated them like gods. Women streamed to them, seeking their company.

Flying those planes was dangerous, especially since the single engine of the craft sat in the front of the pilot. Fuel lines snaked through the cockpit, and a direct hit in aerial combat could turn a plane into an inferno. Even though the pilot could eject, the seconds it took him to hit the release lever could leave his whole face burned—melted into a mass of unrecognizable flesh.

Peter Foster's plane was hit by enemy fire. An explosion burned his face horribly. Peter knew of pilots who returned to England with such wounds; often their wives, unable to deal with their physically destroyed husbands, would divorce them. Peter was not married, but had a girlfriend who came to the hospital and saw how badly he had been burned. Without hesitating, she made the decision not to leave him, assuring him she'd stay by his side. They were later married in the hospital. Foster said, "She became my mirror, and she gave me a new image of myself. Even now, regardless of how I feel, when I look at her, she gives me a warm loving smile telling me I'm okay." [3]

Whom do you know who might look at you and say, "You are a mirror in my life, and when I look at you it inspires me and lifts me up and makes me want to do better?" Who would write down your name? Would your kids? Would your spouse? Would any employees at work? Be loyal in your relationships. Loyalty like that reaps tremendous rewards in returned love and friendship.

GET CLOSE TO THOSE WHOM YOU CAN TRUST

Proverbs 25:9 (NCV) says, "If you have an argument with your neighbor, don't tell other people what was said." Verse 10 follows up, "Whoever hears it might shame you, and you might not ever be respected again." Proverbs 11:13 (NIV) adds, "A gossip betrays a confidence, but a trustworthy man keeps a secret."

We share confidences daily. And yet, when they are broken, we can be deeply wounded.

What's so deadly about breaking a confidence? When you break a confidence you break trust, and trust is the foundation of good, solid relationships. If you break a trust, the relationship can be damaged for life. Do you know anyone you can trust with the deepest secrets of your life? Those people know you at the very heart and core of your being and should become your greatest confidants. And they will trust you with their secrets.

I like the title of John Powell's book *Why Am I Afraid to Tell You Who I Am?* In it he writes, "I am afraid to tell you who I am, because if I tell you who I am, you may not like who I am, and it's all that I have."

Which gender is best at sharing their lives with someone else: male or female? A study done some time ago by a British sociologist named Marion Crawford found that men, especially middle-aged men, considered relationships differently than women do. Women talked about trust and confidentiality; men talked about things they could do together such as enjoy football, basketball, baseball, or work on a car. Women tend to be more personal and trustworthy.[4] Though I'm not trying to say that men aren't equally trustworthy, by nature men are less willing to share their lives openly than women are.

I had two friends in high school, Bob Bilyeu and Dave Stewart, who touched me deeply in this way. I could authentically open up my life with them. We could talk about anything. I could easily discuss things that troubled me, doubts about myself or God, or relationship problems. We held each other accountable for what we were doing with our lives. Through those relationships, I became able to stand against temptation and problems.

DEVELOP HONEST COMMUNICATION

Proverbs 27:6 (NIV) says, "Wounds from a friend can be trusted, but an enemy multiplies kisses." An enemy will tell you all kinds of good things you enjoy hearing, but a good friend will offer you words that can make your life better. Chapter 28:23 (NIV) says, "He who rebukes a man will in the end gain more favor than he who has a flattering tongue."

How do you rebuke somebody without injuring him or her? How do you speak hard words to your spouse and live to tell about it? How do you tell off your kids and not run them off? You must do it honestly but also saturate the words with love and trust. Remember: Honesty is not a virtue when you forget love and trust. Some people say they just "tell it like it is." But if this includes no trust, love, and caring for the person spoken to, it comes off as nastiness.

My first job as a youth was as our church custodian. I thought I was doing a pretty good job—until I went to church one Sunday morning. Our church only had about thirty-five members, so everyone knew everyone else, and we all knew the tasks each person performed in the church.

On that Sunday morning, I vividly remember one of the ladies of the church wiping her glove-clad hand across the pew and looking at it. Then she stared at me, saying, "Well, it looks like the custodian did not do such a good job this week."

I was not highly motivated to go back and clean the church again. I felt put on the spot and judged.

On the other hand, I also remember a good friend I had when I first started to preach. I have to admit that many of my first messages were pathetic. My friend, though, by way of encouragement, would tell me things that I needed to change in my messages. I didn't want to hear it; I didn't like to hear it. Sometimes it was painful to hear. But I knew without any doubt he cared for me and wanted me to do better. This made all the difference in the world. Honest communication must be sweetened with a lot of love, care, and trust.

Bring Out the Best in Each Other

I love Proverbs 27:17 (NIV): "As iron sharpens iron, so one man sharpens another." Have you ever watched a butcher slide a big knife against an iron file to sharpen it? When you sharpen a big knife, you must hold it the right way or you'll dull it. In the same way, seek friends who can make you sharper in your walk with God.

In high school I had three very close friends. We spent much time together, joking, but also sharpening one another's character through honest communication. As I look back on those formative years, besides my parents, these three fellows strengthened my character most. They spoke honest words that sometimes didn't go down sweet but changed me for the better.

In contrast, I remember my eighth-grade year, too. It was my worst year in school. That year, some kids influenced me to skip school, not do my work, and rebel against my teacher. I was a mess. Fortunately, I drifted away from those guys and fell in with more godly fellows.

Proverbs says we should work to make sure we have people around us who sharpen us to be our very best.

Likewise, 1 Corinthians 15:33 reminds us that bad company corrupts good character. Hanging around with the wrong people can wreck your life.

When I moved to Kansas City, I met Mike Gleason. He had just gotten out of prison. When he was just a young man, he and some others decided to rob a store. Mike was pushed into it and was the driver while the others robbed the store. The boys inside ended up killing the clerk, and, as a result, Mike was sent to prison for most of his life. I invited Mike to the little country church I pastored to tell the young people how bad company corrupts good character. I still remember his sad eyes. But his heart was good because in prison he came to believe in Jesus. He was set on a new road by the work of God's Spirit through people who sharpened him.

BE SENSITIVE TO OTHERS' FEELINGS

This is where you find the Bible so relevant and practical. Proverbs 25:17 (NCV) says, "Don't go to your neighbor's house too often; too much of you will make him hate you." In other words, be sensitive to other people's schedules and needs. Don't take too much advantage of a friendship.

Proverbs 25:20 (TLB) says, "Being happy-go-lucky around a person whose heart is heavy is as bad as stealing his jacket in cold weather, or rubbing salt in his wounds." When friends become close, they often feel what the other feels. That's empathy. Such people know when to rejoice with you as well as when to just sit quietly with you and share your pain.

Can you read how your spouse feels? How about your children? If they come home from a terrible day at school and begin to tell you about it, how do you respond? Do you say, "Why that's nothing. You should have been in school when I was your age. I had to walk ten miles in the snow." Be careful. You may be driving your children away through insensitivity to their feelings and needs.

Are you sensitive to those whose paths you cross in the marketplace? Are you able to let them know you understand their feelings? That's what Proverbs teaches. Anyone training to become a leader must learn to feel what the people are feeling if they are going to lead them.

My wife, Charlene, has an unusual ability to look into people's eyes and know if they're tired, troubled, or not well. So many times on the way home from church, she'll say to me, "How did you think so-and-so looked tonight? She seemed to be a little troubled."

Often she'll get home and call the person to talk and find out if he or she needs some encouragement or help. It's a beautiful quality.

ALWAYS BE READY TO FORGIVE

Proverbs 17:9 (NCV) says, "Whoever forgives someone's sin makes a friend." Conflict will eventually invade every relationship you have. Author Alan McGinnis put it this way: "Sooner or later, in any friendship, someone will be wronged. In a weak moment, the beloved will desert us, or severely criticize us, or embarrass us, or walk away from us. And if we allow ourselves to dwell on those misdeeds, the relationship is doomed."[5]

Why should you forgive? McGinnis points out, "Bitterness is an attitude that eats away at us like acid. Not only does our bitterness slop out on others around us and corrode our relationships, it also eats away at our own souls."[6]

The price of forgiveness is great. In fact, forgiving someone who has hurt you deeply, especially if that person is close to you, could be much more difficult than forgiving someone who is just an acquaintance. I believe the greatest challenge we ever face in life is to forgive someone who has hurt us deeply. If it will cost you dearly to forgive them, why do it? Because the cost of not forgiving them is much greater.

God commands us to forgive each other, just as He has forgiven us. When we disobey God on this issue, our unforgiving spirit erodes us on the inside as much as relationships are eroded on the outside.

I remember an angry, bitter woman who came into the office one day. She was facing much conflict in her home. She could be such a sweet person and then suddenly erupt like a volcano and become vicious. She had never dealt with the issue of anger, and she never saw herself as being angry. It was always someone else's fault. I was sad that I never saw her resolve the problem.

THE DEAREST FRIEND

Here's one last thing for you to ponder in the area of relationships. It's about your friendship with Jesus. Author Oswald Chambers says, "The dearest friend on earth is a mere shadow compared with Jesus Christ."[7]

Who is your best friend on earth?

More than anything else that you can gain from this book, I want you to know Jesus as your very best friend. Meeting Him in salvation is only the beginning. As we get to know Jesus better and give up the control of our lives to Him, our friendship deepens. We learn to trust Jesus, and He brings a deep joy and sense of purpose into our lives. Our relationship with Him is the greatest relationship of all.

Even if all your other relationships on earth are in good shape, happy, and fulfilling, make sure your eternal relationship with Jesus is also in good shape, happy, and fulfilling. It's the most important thing you can do every day of your life.

CHAPTER 5

THE
MARRIAGE
THAT MAKES IT

Building a Healthy, Strong Relationship

By wisdom a house is built,
and through understanding it is established.

PROVERBS 24:3 NIV

If you work on a computer, you probably would identify with this mythical request for technical support that I found on the Internet.

"Last year I upgraded Girlfriend 1.0 to Wife 1.0 and noticed the new program began taking up a lot of space and valuable resources. No mention of this phenomenon was included in the product brochure. In addition, Wife 1.0 installs itself into all other programs launched during system initiation, where it monitors all other system activities. Applications such as Poker 10.3 and Beer Bash 2.5 no longer run, crashing the system whenever selected. I am unable to purge Wife 1.0 from my system. I'm thinking about going back to Girlfriend 1.0, but un-install does not work on this program. Can you help me?"

We may chuckle at this, but let's face it: We live in a society that is not very marriage-friendly. It actually costs more in taxes to be married than to be single. Sitcoms and many other TV programs often offer antimarriage content. Seldom do you find a model of a good marriage in the media. Our society has become skeptical of marriage as a lifelong commitment.

The number of U.S. adults married is declining. Statistically fewer adult couples are marrying than twenty years ago.[1] In recent years, divorce and never-married people living together climbed upward. Such statistics show us that people are willing to forgo the traditional marriage route and try out life as single, divorced, or just living together without true commitment. It also demonstrates that our society is willing to raise children in unstable family environments. Where do we turn for help in building healthy, strong marriages in a time when people are valuing marriage less and less?

The Book of Proverbs gives us great technical support on how to succeed in this part of our lives. Let's look at six principles from Proverbs that will help our relationships with our spouses. Of course, you can apply these principles to other relationships including neighbors, coworkers, and even Jesus.

GET A GOOD UNDERSTANDING OF YOUR MATE

Proverbs 24:3 (NIV) says, "By wisdom a house is built, and through understanding it is established." 1 Peter 3:7 (NASB) offers a comparable idea: "You husbands in the same way, live with your wives in an understanding way." What does *understanding* mean? Let's see how the word is used in a few other places in the Bible.

In 1 Kings 4:29 (NIV) we find, "God gave Solomon wisdom

and very great insight, and a breadth of understanding." Here the word *understanding* means *discernment,* the ability to see beneath the surface of things and to the very heart of a matter or a person.

Psalm 78:72 (NIV) adds, "And David shepherded them with integrity of heart; with skillful hands he led them." The word *skillful* is the same Hebrew word as the one translated *understanding.* To live with someone in an understanding way means you can discern his or her needs. The word *skillful* adds to it by suggesting that we meet their needs in an effective way and a learned way. We don't waste time spinning wheels, trying this, trying that, but we hit the need on the head the first time we try.

Let me ask: How well do you understand your mate?

Albert Einstein's wife was once asked if she understood her husband's theory of relativity. She replied, "No, but I understand Dr. Einstein." Which was more important, after all?

What, then, do you need to understand about your mate?

First, understand your mate's personality. This is so important because personality never really changes; it's a God-given characteristic. If you've been married forty or fifty years, you probably have a fairly keen understanding of your mate's personality. But for those who are considering marriage, who are dating, or who are newlyweds, you might believe you can change the other person's personality. It's a typical idea many young people have. Let me tell it to you straight: It won't happen!

According to research, your personality begins forming before you're born. While you're knitted together in your mother's womb, not only have all of your organs, cells, and tissues come together, but part of your personality has also been shaped and coded, even before birth. You won't be able to change something as ingrained as the very cells of your mate's body.

I used to think I could change a person's personality if I simply spent enough time with him or her. I soon realized I could change many things about a person, but not the personality. This has happened a lot with staff people. Sometimes when we would hire someone, I had misgivings about the person's personality. I would hire him or her anyway and try to change the person. This almost always led to disaster.

A second aspect of understanding our mates is understanding their values. This can be tricky because values do change. When you're newly married, your wife may value you more than anything, but then comes baby number one, and you may lose rank quickly. Try to maintain a deep understanding of what is important to your spouse. When that becomes important to you, too, you can serve your spouse more effectively and lovingly.

How about goals? What is your mate striving for? Could you write down at least two of his or her goals? Part of your job is to help your spouse achieve those goals.

When I first came to Pleasant Valley, the church where I now pastor, I did not want my wife forced into too much church involvement. I intentionally worked with her, asking myself, *How did God design her? What goals does she have that I can help her achieve?* I think if you really love someone, you will help them reach their goals. Charlene was always very interested in education. She established different goals over the years: first to teach and later to be a principal. She worked toward her master's degree and did other things in education that I encouraged because I knew that was her goal and ambition. I cautioned her against becoming immersed in things just because the activity needed someone to be involved but was not what she really wanted to do.

You must also seek to understand your spouse's needs. Needs also change throughout life. Author and psychologist Larry Crabb says, "People have one basic personal need which requires two kinds of input for its satisfaction. The most basic need is the sense of personal worth, an acceptance of oneself as a whole, real person. Two required inputs are significance and security. My experience suggests that although men and women need both kinds of input, for men the primary route to personal worth is significance, and for women the primary route is security."[2]

Which one would you pick? I think most men value significance, while women choose security. Do you know your spouse's changing needs? A simple exercise might be for both of you to write down your top five needs and share them with each other. When you understand your spouse's needs, you can meet those needs much more effectively.

HAVE A CLEAR VISION FOR YOUR MARRIAGE

Proverbs 29:18 (NASB) says, "Where there is no vision, the people are unrestrained" or, as the King James Version says, "Where there is no vision, the people perish."

What is vision? Vision is a compelling picture of the future that drives everything within you toward achieving that vision. Do you have a compelling picture of the future of your marriage? Most successful people in business have a clear vision of where they want their business to go. Apply that same principle to your marriage.

In his book *The Triumphant Marriage,* Neil Clark Warren researched successful marriages and came up with ten secrets to a triumphant marriage. The first secret he spoke of was: *Dream a Dream. Construct a Vision of Everything You Believe Your Marriage Can Be.* He says, "At the center of all this dreaming and planning is a constantly recurring theme: 'I want the future to be good for you. If it is not good for you, it cannot be good for us. Whatever is healthy and good for you, we will find a way to make it work in our life together.' "[3]

I've seen so many people get caught up in their careers and have great vision, yet they never involve their spouses. Such people get into trouble. Develop a vision of how to achieve your goals and dreams together as a couple and you will succeed.

My dad was a great visionary, but he always included my mom in the decision-making process. I don't recall his making any decisions in our business or anything else without including her. No surprises happened around our house. He constantly talked through his vision and desires with her.

FOCUS ON COMMUNICATION

You can't talk about relationships without focusing on communication. I recently read about an Illinois man who left his snowbound street for a vacation in Florida. His wife, on a business trip herself, planned to meet him the next day. When he reached his hotel, he sent her an E-mail. Unfortunately, he missed one letter in the address. The E-mail went instead to an elderly woman who had just lost her husband the day before. When the grieving widow read the message, she fell over dead. Her family rushed into the room at the sound of the crash and saw this note on the screen.

> *Dearest wife, just got checked in and everything's pre-*
> *pared for your arrival tomorrow. Your loving husband.*
> *P. S. It sure is hot down here.*

Proverbs 18:21 (NIV) says, "The tongue has the power of life and death."

What you say to your spouse impacts him or her. Make sure your words are uplifting and constructive rather than destructive. Build your loved one's self-esteem with kind, loving words. Don't destroy it with downgrading, mean words.

Norman Wright has written *The Power of a Parent's Words*, a book that helps parents communicate better with their children. He claims unkind words will batter the inside of a child like physical blows bruise the outside. That's why it's called verbal abuse.

And communication isn't just the words we use. Only about 7 percent of our communication comes through the actual words. Thirty-eight percent of meaning is related to the tone in which we speak. "Honey, don't," can drip off your lips sweetly and kindle warm feelings, but a sharp "Honey! Don't!" gives another message.

Surprisingly, much of our communication is received through unspoken body language.[4] The nonverbal ways we communicate—a look, a gesture, a body movement—tell more than the other two elements combined. After awhile in your marriage, your spouse can simply look at you, and you know you're in trouble.

Wright continues, "You may have grown up with parents who used words as weapons, and you hoped you wouldn't do the same with your children. But you will probably repeat the same pattern in some way—unless you become the transition person to break the pattern and develop healthy patterns of communication."[5]

Were you raised in a verbally abusive home? If so, you may reproduce the same trend. How can you break the cycle?

Two thoughts: First, admit it's a problem. Second, ask for help. You can become that "transitional" person Wright speaks of, changed under the power of God's leading in your life. Such changes can greatly impact your family, but few people can make the change all by themselves. Seek professional counseling if you have a tendency to abuse.

Focusing on God's Word can also help. "Do not let any unwholesome talk come out of your mouths, but only what is helpful for building others up according to their needs, that it may benefit those who listen" (Ephesians 4:29 NIV).

Continuing with another element of communication, look at what Proverbs 12:25 (NIV) says: "An anxious heart weighs a man down, but a kind word cheers him up."

To illustrate the power of the kind word, I love the story Benjamin West tells about how he became an artist. "One day his mother went out, leaving him in charge of his little sister Sally. In his mother's absence, he discovered some bottles of colored ink, and, to amuse her, he began to paint Sally's portrait. In doing so, he made quite a mess of things. . .numerous ink splotches here and there. When his mother returned, she saw the mess but said nothing about it. She deliberately looked beyond all that as she picked up the piece of paper. Smiling, she exclaimed, 'Why, it's Sally!' She then stooped and kissed her son. From that time on, Benjamin West would say, 'My mother's kiss made me a painter.' "[6]

Every time I think about this story I wonder how I would have responded if I'd been Benjamin's parent? As a perfectionist, would I have even noticed the picture? Or would I have been too focused on the mess? What would you have done? Just remember the Scripture, "An anxious heart weighs a man down, but a kind word cheers him up."

Can you say the encouraging word at just the right time? Benjamin West's mother knew that right time, and it made his whole career. Proverbs 15:1 (NIV) says, "A gentle answer turns away wrath, but a harsh word stirs up anger." Which are you best at—the gentle answer or the harsh word? "Anger" is only one letter away from "danger."

Author Neil Clark Warren says, "Anger expressed aggressively in a therapist's office may actually reinforce aggressive tendencies."[7] Our flying off the handle often creates more anger. In fact, a study of American domestic violence titled "Behind Closed Doors" found that "80 percent of couples who abuse each other verbally end up in physical combat."[8] This report says that if we let our anger out in the wrong way, it will ruin our marriage, alienate our children, and get us fired. I've seen this happen.

My grandfather was a wonderful man, but he had an anger problem. He became volatile at times. At one point, he had an argument with my uncle, his son. It was so violent that my uncle left and never came back. That was a sad part of my grandfather's life and all because he never dealt with his anger problem.

Think about the TV in your home. Researchers show that watching aggression on television—whether on the news programs or crime shows—can actually increase the probability that viewers will act aggressively. We live in an angry society. Terrorism and murder are the extremes, but they're increasing. I've given personality evaluations over the years, and the area that measures anger in these evaluations continues to increase.

When I was in high school, the songs we listened to were about love. I find, though, that many of the songs today are performed with anger in the music. We are appalled when somebody goes into a store or workplace or school and starts shooting. Angry words and gestures breed more anger and violence.

I find some encouragement in Proverbs 16:24 (NIV): "Pleasant words are a honeycomb, sweet to the soul and healing to the bones." This literally means health to the bone marrow. Pleasant words are like honeycomb, sweet to the soul, healing to the bone marrow.

Billy Sunday, a great evangelist of the early twentieth century, said, "Try praising your wife even if it does frighten her at first." Just go ahead and try it.

In contrast, Proverbs 11:9 (TLB) says, "Evil words destroy." It's a short verse but a powerful one.

A husband and wife went into counseling one day. They had been at each other's throats. The counseling session went right over the husband's head, because when they got back to the car, he said, "Well, did what the counselor said about tact and consideration finally get through your thick skull?"

KEEP TRUSTING YOUR SPOUSE

Proverbs 20:6 (NIV) reads, "Many a man claims to have unfailing love, but a faithful man who can find?" A faithful man is rare.

This is also true about women. Look at Proverbs 31:10–11 (TLB): "If you can find a truly good wife, she is worth more than precious gems! Her husband can trust her, and she will richly satisfy his needs."

Why is trust so important? First, trust builds confidence—confidence in the relationship, confidence in your mate, and confidence in yourself. Much of our self-esteem comes from what we assume a person closest to us thinks of us.

Second, trust builds closeness. When we share deep trust, we find deep intimacy.

Again Neil Warren Clark says, "Two people are at their absolute best with each other if they can be their truest, most authentic selves. . . . When you trust another person, you sense that you can afford to be open and entirely yourself. . . . I have discovered that no marriage can be triumphant until both people are able to be fully and freely themselves."[9]

Trust is also so important because it is the foundation of love. I've seen it happen so often. Love grows cold when trust has been broken.

Jesus Christ died for us on the cross and demonstrated His love for us, but this love never becomes real until, in faith, we accept His love. Love can only become genuine when based on trust.

KEEP LOVE ALIVE AND GROWING

How do you do this? I turn to Proverbs 3:3 (NIV): "Let love and faithfulness never leave you; bind them around your neck, write them on the tablet of your heart." Never let go of love and faithfulness. Hold on to them, because love can grow cold and die.

I like to remind couples of this when I perform a wedding ceremony. Honestly, I think most of the time it goes right over their heads because they stand there looking at one another with stars in their eyes. But occasionally something registers. I also tell them that about five to ten years from now, they can be more in love than they are now, and this goes over the top of their heads, too. They think, *I could never be more in love than I am now.* I'm serious, though. It happened to me and to many others I know.

How do you keep love from growing cold, and how do you make it grow? Consider Proverbs 5:18–19 (NCV): "Be happy with the wife you married when you were young. She gives you joy, as your fountain gives you water. She is as lovely and graceful as a deer." Now read this next phrase, "Let her love always make you happy."

In other words, her love should make you come back for more, like the need you have every day for nourishment and refreshment. You can eat and eat until you think you are going to explode, yet about this time tomorrow, you'll be hungry and need to be fed again. The love relationship must be fed and refreshed every day. Solomon goes on to say, "Let her love always hold you captive" (NCV).

What destroys that captivity? Routine. Can you remember when your mate first called you "honey" or "sweetie" or whatever? I can. I melted in my tracks, it felt so good. But what happens to the word "honey" after a few years? "Do" is usually the next word, isn't it? It doesn't have nearly the ring it had years ago because routine can destroy what once seemed so magnetic and powerful.

Resolve Conflict Quickly

Proverbs 10:12 (NCV) says, "Hatred stirs up trouble, but love forgives all wrongs." Again, Proverbs 16:6 (NCV) adds, "Love and truth bring forgiveness of sin." Conflict is a fact of life. If you don't deal with it, it will deal with you. I like what Ruth Bell Graham says: "If there is never conflict, one of you is not necessary." David Augsburger, in his book *Caring Enough to Confront*, says, "Conflict is natural, normal, neutral, and sometimes even delightful. It can turn into painful or disastrous ends, but it doesn't need to. Conflict is neither good nor bad, right nor wrong. Conflict simply is. How we view, approach, and work through our differences does—to a large extent—determine our whole life pattern."[10]

How do you resolve conflict? Here are four guidelines I've often used in working through conflict.

First, carefully choose your battles. Some issues are not worth the fight. If your mate wants to buy something, and you doubt the need for it, sometimes it's best to say go ahead and buy it rather than fight about it.

Second, don't let pride keep you from yielding. I've seen people dig their heels in purely out of the pride not to give an inch, and they paid a much bigger price trying to win that one battle while they lost the rest of the war.

Third, be willing to agree to disagree. You won't agree on everything. Realize that both you and your spouse will have to give on some issues.

Last, be willing to forgive, which means bearing the cost. A happy marriage is the union of two good forgivers.

Some friends of mine struggled greatly in a second marriage

for each. To me, it looked like they weren't going to make it. The first thing they accepted, though, was the challenge of their relationship. They came to a deep conviction that God had brought them together. In time, they realized forgiveness was the answer as they had hurt each other badly in the first days of their relationship. As they forgave each other, their marriage flourished.

Marriage takes work, practice, and time for living and learning as we make mistakes. But the dividends pay greatly for you and your spouse, as well as your children as they see love and commitment modeled.

Take to heart these six principles from Proverbs, and you will surely succeed in building the kind of home God honors and you enjoy.

CHAPTER 6

PARENTING
THAT DRAWS KIDS TO GOD

The Proverbs' Four-Point Plan

The righteous man leads a blameless life;
blessed are his children after him.

PROVERBS 20:7 NIV

February 1998 was a memorable time in my life—both my father and my mother died within a short period of time. I prayed for them intensely during their illnesses, but they went to be with the Lord. I wondered how I should pray after they were gone. Then it dawned on me—just give thanks to God for my parents.

Since then I have opened my prayer journal and given thanks to God for the rich heritage my parents gave me.

Maybe your parents didn't provide such a good heritage for you. Let me encourage you: You can still be an effective parent. Take an honest look at the way you were raised and consider what your parents did right and what mistakes they made. With hard work, encouragement, and strength from the Lord, you can break away from negative patterns and leave a great legacy for your children to follow.

Wisdom from the Book of Proverbs can help us as we parent. Let's look at four points.

BE A GOOD EXAMPLE

Proverbs 20:7 (NIV) says, "The righteous man leads a blameless life; blessed are his children after him."

One key to positive and effective parenting is simply being a good example. Parents demonstrate values more than they explain or teach them. For instance, a pastor was called to a home where the father was having some trouble with his son. The trouble included drugs and honesty issues. During this conversation, the telephone rang. The call was for the husband, but he instructed his wife to say he was not at home. I wonder how his boy learned to lie?

Many people call into work saying they are ill when they aren't. It may not seem like a big deal at the time, but their children are watching and learning. No matter what you tell your children, your example will be imprinted on their lives.

How can we be a righteous example for our kids? When Solomon writes about righteousness sixty-six times in Proverbs, he's not talking about being a perfect person. He's talking about having a passion to do and be what is right. To be righteous involves two things: what you do and what you are. It's not just in the doing; it's also in the being.

Look again at Proverbs 20:7 (NIV): "The righteous man leads a blameless life." The New American Standard Bible says, "A righteous man. . .walks in his integrity." Such a man is solid through and through, or the same through and through.

Ralph Waldo Emerson said, "What you are speaks so loud I cannot hear what you say." My parents were not perfect, but my parents had a passion to do and be what was right. In that respect, parents become the greatest source of moral education and teaching in our world. It can't start with the schools or the churches. The home is where most moral teaching will occur.

I remember hearing of graduate students who were asked where they received most of their ideas on morals and religion. They said it was at home. Where in the home? "During conversation at family mealtime." This may be because in those casual eating times you were at your best or at your worst. During this time, your conversation embeds lifelong morals and religious teachings in your children.

Look at the last part of Proverbs 20:7 (NIV): "Blessed are his children after him." Such children are blessed to have parents who are a righteous example of godliness. However, it's no guarantee that our kids will be godly. The children still have free will and may go their own way. But parents who are righteous and lead a blameless life will greatly impress their children for God.

Proverbs 14:26 (TLB) says, "Reverence for God gives a man deep strength; his children have a place of refuge and security." Deep faith and reverence toward God bring security into a child's life.

I can remember not being able to find my dad at the end of the day after I had worked at our little general store in southwest Missouri. I finally found him at the little church behind our store. He was sitting on the front steps talking with God.

I saw that my father had a close walk with God, and that brought a lot of security to my life. My parents' reverence for

God filtered down and made me feel safe, loved, and encouraged. My father didn't necessarily instruct me about this, but my parents' trust in God still made me feel secure.

GIVE WISE INSTRUCTION

Proverbs 1:8 (NIV) says, "Listen, my son, to your father's instruction and do not forsake your mother's teaching."

People have told me they don't feel they have the right to try to guide their child in religious matters. Sometimes they say they want their children to choose a church that fits them without any parental influence.

This theory reminds me of a story I heard about the English poet Samuel Taylor Coleridge and his response to a man who didn't believe in giving children religious instruction because he didn't want to prejudice their minds. Coleridge changed the subject abruptly and asked the man if he would like to see his garden. So they walked outside, but there was nothing but a patch of weeds. The man said, "This is not a garden!" Then Mr. Coleridge told him, "Well, you see, I did not want to infringe on the liberty of the garden in any way. I was just giving the garden the freedom to choose its own production."

The man understood what Coleridge was saying. Parents have a tremendous responsibility to direct their children by instructing them morally and religiously. Very few people left to their own devices will find the way God has for them.

Proverbs 7:1 (NIV) amplifies it even more: "My son, keep my words and store up my commands within you." How we teach our children is important. Every one of us is born with a conscience. The conscience acts like a compass inside of us. You can shake a compass and the needle will go every direction, but when you lay it down, it will always point north.

When the conscience within us is programmed properly, it will always point in the right direction. In *Meet Your Conscience,* Warren Wiersbe says, "Conscience is that inner faculty that indicates to us whether our actions are right or wrong."[1] You can argue with your conscience, you can defile it, you can harden it but never get rid of it.

The conscience within you, however, is only dependable if it is programmed properly. If your conscience is hardened against God, you can do things contrary to what God wants you to do, and it will not bother you a bit. Sometimes a life of continuous, purposeful rebellion against God can harden our consciences and warp our compasses. Whenever we violate what our conscience tells us, we harden it. Eventually, it can become useless.

As parents, we must be a channel that God's Spirit can work through to program our children's consciences. Proverbs 13:1 (NIV) says, "A wise son heeds his father's instruction, but a mocker does not listen to rebuke." Kids have a choice. They can have the best parents in the world and still break their parents' hearts by their attitudes and actions. It is puzzling when you see parents who have walked with God, parented the very best they knew how, and then their children turned out to be heartbreakers.

This tells me that children can decide whether or not they will follow the instructions that God gives them through their parents. The responsibility for the success of the parenting process is not totally on the parents, it's also on the choices children make. If a child chooses to disobey even a godly, loving parent, that is his or her choice, even though it may be wrong.

Our daughter was very strong-willed. If she planned to do something wrong, she would tell us right to our faces what she wanted to do. She was ready to go to work one day, all dressed up, and this young guy came by on a motorcycle to take her to work. I said, "Kelly, I don't want you to do that."

She said, "I know you don't want me to do that, but I'm doing it anyway." And she walked out.

About five minutes later, she stepped back in the door. Her fine clothes were ripped to shreds. The guy looked the same. Their motorcycle had hit some loose gravel, and the driver lost control. They were thrown into the grass. When she walked back into the house, she said, "Don't say 'I told you so.'" She went to her room and changed, and that was the last I heard of it.

DISCIPLINE WISELY

How do you do that? Discipline is a challenge in every home and at every age. Dr. Ross Campbell says, "In disciplining our children there are no simple answers or easy formulas."[2] If there were just one formula when a child misbehaves, you could go to a book and say here's what you do, one, two, three, four. But. . . there's no guaranteed way to discipline your children so they'll automatically come out all right. There's no magic formula.

Each parent often must try several different strategies before finding the one that works with his child.

I think about Franklin Graham, who had godly parents in Billy and Ruth Graham. Yet Franklin was a rebel. No magic formula made him turn out to be what they wanted. The end result, though, was that he came back to the Lord and has turned out to be a tremendous spiritual leader.

Discipline is also a challenge because it is plain hard work. Psychologist and author Dr. James Dobson discusses this in his book *Parenting Is Not for Cowards*. Many times we parents would much rather let children do what they want because it's the easiest route. But remember the path of least resistance is hardly ever the best path. It is hard work to discipline a child at any age.

The apostle Paul offers us insight for the third reason discipline is so hard. We start out with a fallen, evil nature. He says in Romans 3:23 (NIV), "For all have sinned and fall short of the glory of God."

As parents, we must understand that we have a flawed product on our hands. Every person is born into the world with a nature prone to do wrong. You don't have to sit down and teach your child how to mess up, do you? You don't have to teach any two-year-old child to be selfish. No, we must teach them the opposite—to share.

Jesus said in Matthew 7:13–14 that the path to destruction is wide and many are on it, while the path to eternal life is narrow and few find it. It is at the very core of our fallen nature to drift toward the way of destruction.

What then should we do as parents? Here's some wisdom from Proverbs 13:24 (NIV) about the issue. "He who spares the rod hates his son, but he who loves him is careful to discipline him." It gets better in Proverbs 22:15 (NIV): "Folly is bound up in the heart of a child, but the rod of discipline will drive it far from him."

Proverbs 23:13 says, "Do not withhold discipline from a

child; if you punish him with the rod, he will not die" (NIV). Surprise, verse 14 (NIV): "Punish him with the rod and save his soul from death."

Please understand this has nothing to do with child abuse. These verses can be misunderstood. There is a stark difference between discipline and punishment.

Discipline is teaching your child the way he or she should go and then encouraging and even rewarding him or her to move in that direction. Discipline actually means encouragement or training. Sometimes it may be a hug, a smile, or it may be a positive statement, such as, "I'm so pleased at the way you picked up your toys today." Or, "I'm so pleased at the way you put all your clothes in the closet." Discipline involves demonstrating the way to go and then giving encouragement to go in that direction.

Punishment is a part of discipline and is what we usually think of as "discipline." Punishment is causing pain for wrongdoing. Many of these verses talk about "the rod." What's that about? Here's what psychologist and author Kevin Leman says: "Perhaps the most misused (not to mention misquoted) verse in the Bible is 'Spare the rod, spoil the child.' The actual text reads, 'He who spares the rod hates his son, but he who loves him is careful to discipline him' (Proverbs 13:24 (NIV). The Jews believed in discipline, but when biblical writers used the word *rod* they were thinking more of correction and guidance than of hitting and beating. For example, the shepherd used his rod not to beat his sheep but to guide them."[3]

Leman says spanking is sometimes necessary, but an overuse of it is dangerous and can cause rebellion down the road in the child's life.

Let's say "the rod" can mean anything causing discomfort. For small children, a time-out might be the temporary discomfort. We don't have to beat them with an actual stick. In this regard, punishment should reflect the age and needs of each child.

Here are several guidelines:

First, punish thoughtfully with love. I would really encourage you never to punish your child when you are angry, irritated, or hurt. Wait until you calm down. The younger the child is, the sooner you should levy the punishment, so he or she remembers what you are punishing him or her for. This will give you time to think about your options. I've made mistakes when punishing my children because I did not stop to think about what needed to be done.

Second, make sure the punishment fits the behavior. If a child does not do his or her homework and continues to procrastinate, several options are available. How about being grounded for a month? What about taking away television privileges? A path some parents have chosen that I think is effective is sitting down with your children when they're having trouble with something and asking, "What do you think your punishment should be?" My children and I have often come up with a unique and powerful punishment by working together on it.

The important thing is that every child and situation is different. You must decide the best way to handle each incident. Simply make sure the discomfort fits the misbehavior.

What if children are defiant? What do you do if a child looks you right in the eye and flatly says, "I'm not going to do it!" I've always thought it wise to reserve spanking for such defiant moments. And it has worked, too.

A punishment should also fit the child's temperament. For example, if you have a highly social son who loves being around people, send him to his room for misconduct. This will be uncomfortable for him.

On the other hand, what about the shy kid who is reserved and introverted? If you send him to his room, he'll think, *This is great! I was wanting to get out of there anyway.* Something else will be more effective.

What about the sensitive child who melts with a stern look? You may never have to spank this child. You may just look at her and have her attention.

Let's talk about spanking for just a minute. When should it be used? Children should never be abused, but at times spanking is necessary. My parents spanked me a few times. I remember my dad had a belt with a hole in the end of it. It hung on the wall in the kitchen. Its very presence had tremendous power, but how do you use something like that?

First, never spank when you're angry. My dad was in charge of the spankings, but he never spanked me when he was angry. When I'd pushed him into a fit about something, he would tell me I would be punished that evening. What a way to ruin a day! Fortunately, by evening my dad was calm and collected and able to clearly communicate to me the reason why I was being punished. My dad would then tell me he loved me and how much he hated to punish me.

Second, never strike a child in the face. My parents never struck me except in the padded place God provided on the backside of the body. Also, there are limits to the power of spanking. In children less than two years old, you're wasting your time. Also, nine or ten years old is a good upper limit on spanking. Don't try to spank a seventeen or eighteen year old, or you might end up on the bottom of the heap.

Moms and Dads, this is a tough one. If you know you made a mistake in a certain punishment, apologize to your child and ask for forgiveness. You will earn respect in the eyes of your children. Sometimes children need to know their parents aren't perfect, either. Letting them see your imperfection also models humility for your children.

BRING OUT THE BEST IN YOUR CHILD

Proverbs 22:6 (NIV) talks about bringing out the best in your child: "Train a child in the way he should go, and when he is old he will not turn from it."

There are many misunderstandings about this verse. Some think it means that if your child is in church or Sunday school regularly, if he learns Bible verses and goes to Christian camps, he'll return to the faith after he sows his inevitable wild oats. Since he will surely stray off into sin during his late teens and early twenties, this verse promises that someday, because of his early Christian training, he'll come back to his roots and to God.

This thinking is false. It's not what the verse is talking about. As I've said before, each child has a choice, and even with great parenting, a child can choose the wrong path and never turn back.

To get the right idea of this verse, look at three words. The first one is the word *train*. What does it mean to train a child? You might be interested to know the original root word for *train* is *the palate as of the mouth or the roof of the gums.* In the verb form, it is the term used for bringing a wild horse to submission by a rope in the mouth.

The term was also used in Solomon's day to describe the actions of a midwife who, soon after helping deliver a child, would dip her finger in the juices of chewed or crushed dates, reach into the mouth of the infant, and massage the gums and the palate to create a sensation of sucking. Then she placed the child in the mother's arms to begin feeding from the mother's breast.

Finally, train also was used to describe thirst.

Each of these definitions shows us that training is about motivating the child to go in a certain direction. We train them when we give them encouragement and the desire to follow our teachings.

How long do you train a child? Certainly you should start at birth, but children grow rapidly. When is a child no longer a child? The word *child* was used to describe Joseph when he was seventeen years old, so childhood, in the minds of the Hebrew writers, extends through adolescence to early adulthood.

A second word to look at from Proverbs 22:6 is the word *way.* In this context it means *the predetermined bent* or *personality* that God has given our children. The verse then means: "Train up a child according to his bent in life."

This is something I missed completely when our first child came along. About the time you get the hang of it with your first child, the second one comes along, and you have to start over, because he has a whole new personality and bent.

I tried to discipline our first child, Kelly, the way my dad had disciplined me. It didn't work. After awhile, I discovered I could not discipline her by the model I'd learned from my dad. I had to discipline her according to the way God had designed her.

Then our son came along. With him, we had to throw away the manual we'd learned with our daughter. My dad's discipline model didn't work with him, either. We had to devise new methods.

Even if you didn't grow up with perfect parents, be encouraged that God can use you in your children's lives. You can point them in the right direction. Take these parenting points from Proverbs, and God will surely lead you day by day in the discipline and training of your children.

Most importantly, stay on your knees in prayer for them every step of the way.

CHAPTER 7

MAKING YOUR
MONEY
WORK FOR YOU

Four Principles on Finance

How much better to get wisdom than gold,
to choose understanding rather than silver!

PROVERBS 16:16 NIV

Something about money makes our adrenaline pump. If you doubt me, just look at the ratings of the TV show *Who Wants to Be a Millionaire?* For awhile, the chance to win that much money really got people excited.

Money is an extremely important part of our lives. The writer of Proverbs must have thought so, too. The book is packed full of verses about money and possessing things. Out of thirty-one chapters in Proverbs, twenty-four say something about money. Sixty-eight verses mention money.

What exactly is money? It's a medium of exchange, but it's really much more than that in our lives. What other words could define money? Power. Value. Evil. Security.

Richard Foster says, "Money is not just a neutral medium of exchange but a 'power' with a life of its own. And very often is a 'power' that is demonic in character."[1]

Fred Smith put it this way: "Money is option. Money brings options, just as poverty eliminates them. While money provides options, it does not supply the ability to choose the right option. That requires character."[2]

As a result, money becomes a spiritual facet of our lives. Every spending decision is a spiritual decision. Gene Getz, a pastor in Texas, says that "God says more about how Christians are to view and use their material possessions than most any other subject."[3]

Here are four principles from the Book of Proverbs about money and finances that I think could significantly change your life.

MONEY ISN'T EVERYTHING

Keep a wise perspective of money. Money isn't everything, but it sure does help you to keep in touch with your children when they get a little older, doesn't it? Look at Proverbs 16:16 (NIV), "How much better to get wisdom than gold, to choose understanding rather than silver!"

What did we say wisdom is? Skill. Wisdom is the skill to use what you know. You can have a great education or vast knowledge, but if you don't have the skill to use it, you don't have wisdom. In the context of money, wisdom provides the skill to manage money without it managing you. Wisdom keeps money in proper perspective.

Money has a way of getting a grip on your life. The temptation to amass money can lead some into materialism—a devotion to material wealth and possessions at the expense of spiritual and intellectual values. I like what Howard Hendricks says: "Materialism has nothing to do with the amount. It has everything to do with the attitude."[4]

Materialism is not just for the extremely wealthy. You can have very few things and still be materialistic. How do you determine if you've become materialistic? Take this little test:

Answer yes or no.

1. I do not have any overdue bills.
2. I do not have any anxiety about money.
3. I manage money well by living according to a budget.
4. I am not preoccupied by the thought of getting rich quick.
5. I do not compare myself to others and what others have and say, "Why not me?"
6. I find contentment in what I already have.
7. I do not think just a little more would make me happier.
8. I am not overcommitted at work.
9. I have time to do God's work.
10. I cheerfully give a tithe to God.

If you can say yes to all ten questions, you probably have a good perspective on money. If you said no on some, I would encourage you to set some goals to turn each "no" into a "yes."

Solomon continues his discussion about money in Proverbs 11:28 (NIV): "Whoever trusts in his riches will fall, but the righteous will thrive like a green leaf."

The first half of that verse reminds us that things and money can give us a false sense of security. The sinking of the *Titanic* taught us an important lesson: We find no security in material things. That huge, luxurious ship represented in many ways a great source of security for people. Many tremendously wealthy people took berths on the *Titanic*. They had a great sense of security, but it was false.

I think of two verses from Proverbs that spell out the attitude some had about the "unsinkable" *Titanic*. Proverbs 18:11 (NASB): "A rich man's wealth is his strong city, and like a high wall in his own imagination." In other words, the security the passengers had when they sailed on the *Titanic* was just in their imaginations. It was not real because they sank. Another verse amplifies that idea: "Riches won't help on the day of judgment" (Proverbs 11:4 NLT).

The value of money changed quickly on the *Titanic*. When that ship began to go down, money became worthless. No one who truly understood the risk ran back into cabins to grab a few more coins or jewels. They left it all behind. It no longer mattered. Only survival mattered. The Bible teaches over and over that riches won't help you when you arrive at the great judgment.

Turning back to Proverbs 11:28 (NIV), note the last part of it: "But the righteous will thrive like a green leaf." What does this mean? Righteousness in the Old Testament did not necessarily mean measuring up to the rules God gave the Hebrews. Righteousness is not perfection. Rather, righteousness is a passion to be rightly related to God and other people, to do and treat others properly and with kindness and respect. That kind of righteousness causes us to thrive. Beware of the false security of stored-up money, and work on those things that are really valuable—your relationship with God and others is the principle.

Watch What You Owe

The second principle about money is to be wise about debt. Proverbs 22:7 (NIV) says, "The rich rule over the poor, and the borrower is servant to the lender." This is a big issue in America. Borrowing has become a way of life. Credit cards have led us to make unbelievable purchases, far beyond our means. Someone hit on the problem when they said, "Many people have discovered that money can't buy happiness, and now they're trying credit cards."

Many people have descended into the bondage of debt because they can't get themselves beyond the monthly crunch of their credit-card bills.

Our church has a ministry called Budget Management. It's a series of classes that help people get out of debt and free from that bondage. We have teachers who lead people in developing the discipline, character, and motivation to work their way out of debt. There is nothing like being set free financially. Many programs, financial planners, and books offer help with budgeting skills and general financial management. If you need help in this area, it's there.

In 1990s, personal bankruptcies began to skyrocket. The biggest reason is the ease of getting credit cards. Almost everyone receives promotions in the mail or telephone calls about signing up for a credit card. Usually the pitch is something like, "You've been preapproved for a credit card. You should know that preapproved status is not easily achieved, but with your excellent financial record, our decision was really very simple. We want you as a card member."

Becoming a card member is as easy as signing your name.

Because of the cards, it's easy to get in debt. Forty-four percent of families have outstanding credit-card debt. In America in 2003, the average person carries nine credit cards, with unpaid balances of about $9,000.[5]

Here's how some people get caught in the credit-card trap. Say you have a $9,000 unpaid balance on a credit-card, and you decide not to spend another dime on it. So you pay the minimum payment of less than $180 a month. How long would it take to pay off that debt at that rate? Thirty years. In the process, with the interest added, you will have spent a total of $64,800. Is that a wise management of money?

Can credit cards be used wisely? Of course, if you follow some simple guidelines.

1. Use your credit card only for budgeted items.
   Never buy something you can't pay for.
2. Pay your credit card off every month. Don't be late, because you'll be charged for that.
3. The first month that you find you can't pay your credit-card bill, cut your card and close your account.

The public debt before 9/11 and the Iraqi war was $5.7 trillion. Our public debt has more than doubled since 1987. The average American today spends $1.03 of every dollar they earn. That means we're just digging ourselves under the debt pile even deeper.

The good news is we're a lot happier today. Right? Not so! Look at this research. "Between 1956 and 1988 the percentage of Americans saying that they were 'pretty well satisfied with their present financial situation' dropped from 42 percent to 30 percent."[6]

Isn't that ironic? The more we have and borrow, the less satisfied we are with what we have. Be wise about debt; pay off those credit cards, and you will find God's blessing, both financially and personally.

INVEST WHAT YOU HAVE

A third financial principle found in Proverbs is to consistently invest money wisely. Look at Proverbs 6:6–8 (NIV): "Go to the ant, you sluggard; consider its ways and be wise! It has no commander, no overseer or ruler, yet it stores its provisions in summer and gathers its food at harvest."

Ants know how to invest. They know how to save and prepare for the future. That's a little ant. Nobody's over these little creatures with a whip, forcing them to do it. But they manage.

Do you have a budget, and do you live by it? If not, why not? Isn't that a pretty simple thing to do? It's not easy, but it's simple. I got an E-mail last week from a college student. He said, "I remember your messages about money and budgeting. Could you please send me that information? I need it." We all need to learn to live within our means.

Proverbs 13:11 (NIV) provides another insight: "He who gathers money little by little makes it grow." We've all heard about the millionaire next door—he never made big sums at once, but he salted his little sums away. You don't have to be super knowledgeable about the stock market. You don't have to have a lot of money. You only have to do two things to practice this verse. It will change your life.

First, consistently set aside some savings every time you get paid. A little girl came up to me after the church service one night, and I said, "Do you get an allowance?"

She said yes. I said, "Do you take a little bit of your money each week and put it in a little piggy bank?"

She said yes, and then after it amounts to a bit, she and her parents take it to the bank so it can draw interest. Even when someone is ten or eleven years old, they can understand this principle.

Second, save like this over a long period of time. What's the result of that? Here's an example of the advantage of having money building on itself, or compounding. If, at the age of twenty, you earn $15,000 a year, and you invest 10 percent for forty-five years, when you retire at sixty-five, you will have $1 million. The sooner you begin, the greater the result. What is amazing is that few people who retire in our society today even come close to that. Yet, the principle has been in the Bible for over three thousand years.

My dad taught me the 10-10-80 plan when I was very young. Give 10 percent to God, save 10 percent, and use the rest to pay the bills. I started that when I had an allowance of fifty cents a week. It was ingrained in me and has become a way of life for me.

LEARN TO GIVE

Practice generosity. You cannot read the Book of Proverbs and miss the verses on giving. Look at Proverbs 11:25 (NASB): "The generous man will be prosperous, and he who waters will himself be watered." The apostle Paul wrote the same thing in 2 Corinthians 9:6 (NIV): "Whoever sows generously will also reap generously."

This principle works throughout life. For example, you give energy, and you will get energy. I exercise every day. Sometimes I'm so tired that I don't want to do it. But I have found that after I've finished that two miles of walking, I am energized.

Another example: You put one grain of corn in the ground, and it grows and yields many more grains in return. Give yourself in friendship to somebody else, and it begins to come back to you in great friendship. Give your time in wise planning, and it will give you some time back. Give your life, and it will begin to give you life back.

Jesus said it this way in Mark 8:35 (NIV): "For whoever wants to save his life will lose it, but whoever loses his life for me and for the gospel will save it."

It's a pretty clear lesson, isn't it? Look at Proverbs 14:31 (NIV): "He who oppresses the poor shows contempt for their Maker, but whoever is kind to the needy honors God." That's a sobering statement. You oppress the poor, and you're in contempt in God's eyes.

How we give to others says a lot about our faith. Do you experience joy in giving? Of course, we should add that giving money won't necessarily mean a return in financial blessings from God. He promises to provide for our needs, and as we give, He will continue to provide. However, the blessing we might receive from giving may be spiritual (such as an increase in our faith) or in some other area of our lives.

When I first moved to Kansas City, I didn't have anywhere to preach, so I just took my old Sears and Roebuck guitar and went down to the City Union Mission. I sang to the guys as they came out of the gutter into the chapel service, which they had to attend before eating soup. We'd just sing for them and worship—and it truly touched my life as I got acquainted with those people who needed help. I believe in some way I was giving to the Lord when I gave my time and my singing to those people who needed the Lord's love.

Let me challenge you to get out of your ivory palace and find a place where you can give to God by helping someone in desperate need.

Proverbs 19:17 (NIV) helps us here: "He who is kind to the poor lends to the LORD." I am amazed at this. Would you like to lend the Lord some money? Do you think He gives good dividends? "He who is kind to the poor lends to the LORD, and he will reward him for what he has done." Would you like to receive rewards from the Lord that will last for eternity? Think about that for a minute.

Remember that though money is a very spiritual item, you can never give enough to get you into heaven. I still find that many people who hope they're going to heaven tell you of all the things they've done. The Bible teaches that you can never do enough to get into heaven. Good deeds will gain God's blessing, but only faith will open the doors of heaven for you.

A Kansas City Chiefs football player named Derrick Thomas died at an early age in an accident. He was known for his wonderful generosity. People praised him constantly and thought highly of him.

I'm sure even God thought he was a nice guy. But I honestly don't know where Derrick Thomas was in relation to the Lord. Had he put his faith in Christ? I don't know. But I do know this: If he's in heaven today, it's not because he gave away a lot of money. It's only because of the amazing, saving grace of Jesus Christ who died on the cross to forgive us of our sins. If Derrick put his faith in Jesus while he was alive, we will see him in heaven someday, and all of his giving will be greatly rewarded. But if he didn't put his faith in Christ, all of that giving hasn't helped him in eternity.

Paul said in Ephesians 2:8–9 (NASB), "For by grace you have been saved through faith; and that not of yourselves, it is the gift of God; not as a result of works, so that no one may boast." Faith is the key. Without it, all of us are lost.

As a child of God and out of respect for what Jesus did for us on the cross, we should strive to be the best servants possible in every area, including money. If we keep a wise perspective about money, keep an eye on debt, consistently invest our money, and give generously, we will be well on our way to honoring the Lord in this area.

CHAPTER 8

TALK

THAT MAKES LIFE WONDERFUL

Using Our Words Wisely

> *The tongue has the power of life and death,*
> *and those who love it will eat its fruit.*

PROVERBS 18:21 NIV

What comes to mind when you hear the word *power?* Strength? Dynamite? Prayer? Do you think about God? Certainly. If you've ever been caught in a tornado, you have an excellent image of power. I remember, when I was a kid, hearing and seeing the power of big locomotives rattling the ground as they roared by.

When you consider relationships, power is probably demonstrated best through our words. For example, say you're attending a baseball game where the outcome is in doubt. Here comes the winning run, and after the dust begins to settle, the umpire yells just two words, "You're out!" That's power.

What about in a courtroom? One word—*guilty*—marks the defining moment. Have you ever heard that sweet word—*benign*—when the doctor steps in from surgery? That's powerful.

Napoleon understood the power of words. Emil Ludwig said half of what Napoleon achieved in his great kingdom was through the power of his words.

In the first three chapters of Genesis, we find two words thirteen times—"God said." "God said," and creation came into being. Creation demonstrates the tremendous power in the words of God.

We have a similar power. Our words can mean life and death in some situations. They can spell success or defeat in others. Let's look at some examples of the power of our words from Proverbs.

1. "The tongue has the power of life and death, and those who love it will eat its fruit" 18:21 (NIV). That's power—to give life or exact death.
2. "The tongue that brings healing is a tree of life, but a deceitful tongue crushes the spirit" 15:4 (NIV). The tongue can heal people or crush their spirit.
3. "Some people have teeth like swords; their jaws seem full of knives" 30:14 (NCV). You've met people like that, haven't you?
4. "The words of a good person give life, like a fountain of water, but the words of the wicked contain nothing but violence" 10:11 (NCV).

Another writer, this time in the New Testament, has much to say about words. You find in James 3:5–6 (NLT): "So also, the tongue is a small thing, but what enormous damage it can do. A tiny spark can set a great forest on fire. And the tongue is a flame of fire. It is full of wickedness that can ruin your whole life." A few words can turn the course of your life into a blazing furnace of destruction. That's power!

In high school, we used to make little clothespins that could shoot a match while lighting it. We were on the bus one day when one of the kids shot one out the window. It was just a small lit match, but we quickly saw a flaming field behind us. James says that is how powerful our words are. One small indiscretion in what you say can lead to big problems, hurt feelings, and misunderstandings. Proverbs is full of verses that tell us how to use our words wisely. Let's look at five guidelines to help us.

THINK FIRST!

The first guideline is to think before we speak. Think through what you will say and what impact you expect it to make. A little forethought can prevent many misdirected words.

We find in Proverbs 17:14 (NCV), "Starting a quarrel is like a leak in a dam, so stop it before a fight breaks out." Just slow down and think before you say anymore and cause a huge problem.

Proverbs 18:13 (NIV) says, "He who answers before listening—that is his folly and his shame." Truly listening to the other person before we speak can prevent us from saying words we later regret.

Another of my favorite reminders in this area is Proverbs 29:20 (NCV): "Do you see people who speak too quickly? There is more hope for a foolish person than for them."

Proverbs 12:18 (NIV) tells us, "Reckless words pierce like a sword, but the tongue of the wise brings healing." Words are another form of power and can go either way. Words, like a sword, can kill, or like a scalpel, can bring healing.

And Proverbs 10:19 (NIV): "When words are many, sin is not absent, but he who holds his tongue is wise."

The verses go on and on. Are you beginning to get the point? Slowing down and thinking about our words before we say them enormously affects how we communicate to those around us. How can we slow down and learn to think first? Through discipline that becomes a habit. When we train ourselves to do a certain task over a period of time, it becomes a learned habit—a normal and natural reaction. For instance, many of us have the habit of buckling our seat belts before we start our cars. We don't even think about it anymore. We just do it. But at one time, I had to train myself to buckle up each time I got in the car. In the same way, after a time of training ourselves to stop and think before speaking, it will become automatic.

KEEP COOL!

A second guideline is to carefully guard your words when you are angry. Proverbs 29:22 (NIV) says, "An angry man stirs up dissension, and a hot-tempered one commits many sins." Anger can cause you to say things that you will deeply regret.

I once heard of a man named George Martin, who tells this story: "I remember a fellow who once wrote a nasty letter to his father. Since we worked in the same office, I advised him not to send it because it was written in a fit of anger. But he sealed it and asked me to mail it. Instead, I slipped it into my coat pocket and kept it until the next day. The following morning he arrived at the office looking very worried.

" 'George,' he said, 'I wish I had never sent that note to my dad yesterday. It hurts me deeply, and I know it will break his heart when he reads it. I'd give fifty dollars to get it back!' Taking the envelope from my pocket, I took it to him and told him what I had done. He was so overjoyed that he actually wanted to give me fifty dollars."

We've all said things in anger we wished we could take back, haven't we? Is anger the problem here? Not necessarily. Anger isn't always bad. In fact, sometimes we should be angry. But in those times we have to watch what we do or say. Ephesians 4:26 (NCV) tells us, "When you are angry, do not sin." When you're angry, just be sure that you're in control and that you don't say some things that could be sinful. Proverbs 14:29 (NIV) helps us with that: "A patient man has great understanding." A patient person who is slow to anger demonstrates great wisdom.

One way to control your anger is to understand your attitude toward yourself. You might say, "What does that have to do with anything?" Neil Clark Warren says, "The first thing to do if you are going to be an expert in handling your anger is to get your self-concept into shape."[1] To take charge of an area of your life, build a solid, positive, healthy self-esteem. It goes a long way.

Here's the way it works. If I don't have a very positive self-concept, I don't feel very good about myself. If I hear someone say something I perceive as insulting and critical, I will become defensive. People with poor self-esteem are easily threatened and will come back at you fighting mad.

On the other hand, if I have a healthy self-esteem and someone says insulting or critical things about me, I won't get knocked off my feet. I probably will think, *Why's he saying that? I know better than that. I know I'm not like that.* I won't try to protect myself by being defensive and will be less likely to lash out in anger. Sometimes controlling my tongue begins with controlling the way that I think about myself.

We also need to understand our level of built-up anger. Be honest. Do you have a high level of anger piled up on the inside? Here's what happens. You get a little bit angry about something and just keep it inside. A little bit later you get angry, and you just stuff it again. You're at work, around the family, with friends, driving in your car, and you just keep shoving your anger down into that little spot in your heart for stored memories.

Now what happens when that little spot gets full? The least little extra pressure and you blow up! *Kaboom!*

Unless you're aware of where your anger level is, you may be ready to blow. You may have been pushing your anger down rather than processing situations and letting go of them. Handle your anger as it arises. Deal with it and speak up, if necessary, in a kind way. Then you won't be ready to explode over trivial matters.

Another good thing to do: Understand your feelings. Do you know when you're getting angry? Can you feel it rising in your mind? If you're very sensitive and understand when you're getting angry and can deal with it immediately, you will be able to control your anger.

Controlling anger is kind of like stopping a locomotive. It's pretty easy to stop it if it is going two miles an hour. But once it is moving fifty, sixty, or seventy miles per hour, you could put a dozen trailer trucks in front of the train, and it would just ram them off the tracks. By dealing with anger at the initial stages, you can control it. But if you allow it to get up to a high level, it controls you.

Not only should we understand our angry feelings, but we should also try to understand why we're angry. Anger usually comes from three different areas: hurt, frustration, or fear. Ask yourself: Am I angry because I am hurt or frustrated or afraid? When we understand why we're angry, we find it easier to control our tongues.

I grew up in a culture that thought anger was wrong. As a result, I always denied I was angry, when I really was. As a result, I stuffed my anger on the inside. Eventually, that caught up with me, and it came out in depression. I have had to learn to identify when I'm angry and admit it and then process it.

SOMETHING TO TALK ABOUT

A third guideline we see in Proverbs is to avoid gossip. Proverbs 20:19 (NCV) says, "Gossips can't keep secrets, so avoid people who talk too much."

What does gossip mean? The Hebrew word for gossip literally means to enlarge or widen or open. Gossips enlarge their mouths. They talk way too much about things they shouldn't be talking about. Gossips not only have big mouths, but they also tend to bring up unpleasant topics and discuss them with others.

It's hard not to listen to gossip. Something about gossip makes us curious. Proverbs 18:8 (NIV) says, "The words of a gossip are like choice morsels; they go down to a man's inmost parts." Something about the lower nature of humans makes gossip appetizing. That's why people pick up tabloid magazines. Even if they don't necessarily believe the reports, they still enjoy reading about other people's problems.

What is even worse about gossip is that once it leaves your mouth, you can never retrieve it—like feathers from a pillow on a windy day. Those feathers might fly hundreds of miles in a short time. To go back and grab all those feathers and put them back in the pillow is like trying to retract gossip. It cannot be done. The guideline is: Avoid all gossip!

You've probably played the game "Telephone," where you line people up and the first one whispers a sentence or two to the next person. This goes on down the line until the last person tells what he or she heard. It's often funny because the message has become so garbled by then.

The game teaches us that gossip often gets completely out of hand when it's passed around a few times.

HONESTY: THE BEST POLICY?

Our fourth guideline on great speech is speaking the truth in love. Proverbs 25:12 (NIV) puts it, "Like an earring of gold or an ornament of fine gold is a wise man's rebuke to a listening ear." Why do you wear jewelry? Most people wear jewelry because they think it makes them look better or more beautiful. Now, look at this verse again. "Like an earring of gold or an ornament of fine gold is a wise man's rebuke to a listening ear." In other words, the purpose of a good, wise rebuke is to make someone more beautiful.

How do you rebuke in love? First, ask yourself why you

want to correct the person. Is it for him or her, or for you? Are you saying something because you want to get it off your chest and tell the person what you think, or do you want to make him or her more beautiful?

Second, if you think you'll get joy out of doing the rebuke, then don't do it. When you're rebuking someone, you should feel the pain even more than he or she does.

Third, have you earned the right to rebuke? Do you have such a relationship with the person that he or she knows you genuinely care? If that person doesn't know how much you care, your rebuke will probably not help him or her.

Last, make the rebuke as positive as possible. Don't just give the person the junk; point him or her in the right direction.

I had a coach in high school who earned our respect by not yelling at us or putting us down but by carefully and directly explaining to us what we were doing wrong and how to correct it. He instructed us. We had a winning team that year because he knew how to build teamwork and help us act as a unit.

On the other hand, we can't just say something nice when it's not true. In fact, one way we sidestep the responsibility of telling someone the truth in love is by flattery. Sincere compliments are great—we should all get in the habit of giving them freely and frequently. But to say something kind with an ulterior motive is not right. Proverbs 26:28 (NIV) says, "A lying tongue hates those it hurts, and a flattering mouth works ruin." Chapter 13:14 (NIV) adds, "The teaching of the wise is a fountain of life, turning a man from the snares of death." So we must make sure our words are true.

Do you remember Christa McAuliffe, the schoolteacher who died in the *Challenger* on that fatal space mission? She said, "I touch the future; I teach."[2] How right she was. I can still remember people who taught me in elementary school and Sunday school. They changed my life. Teachers have the incredible opportunity to mold the lives of children—for good or bad.

We've all had wise teachers in some area of our lives. When you were a child, it might have been your parents, teachers, or coaches. Today it could be a pastor, friend, business associate, or employer. When wise people instruct us, Solomon says it is like a fountain of life for our souls.

SAY SOMETHING GOOD!

The fifth guideline is to consistently give words of encouragement. Let's look again at Proverbs 16:24 (NIV), "Pleasant words are a honeycomb, sweet to the soul and healing to the bones." Pleasant words are like something sweet that goes down to the very core of our being. Chapter 25:11 (NCV) adds this variation: "The right word spoken at the right time is as beautiful as gold apples in a silver bowl." The right words spoken at the right time are more valuable than silver and gold.

Words can change lives. Encouraging words build up, and critical words destroy. Is it any surprise the apostle Paul said something like this in Romans 10:10 (NIV): "For it is with your heart that you believe and are justified, and it is with your mouth that you confess and are saved." Confessing Jesus as Lord literally changes the course of all eternity for your life. "Everyone who calls on the name of the Lord will be saved," (Romans 10:13 NIV). Can you tell me anything more powerful than a confession of faith from the heart?

Words are perhaps the most powerful thing in the world. God created the world with them, we go to heaven by confessing our faith, and we can choose to build or destroy our brothers, sisters, children, and friends by what we say. Take Solomon's advice and be wise with your use of words.

CHAPTER 9

MANAGING YOUR
ANGER
IN AN ANGRY WORLD

Insights into a Powerful Emotion

Anger is cruel and destroys like a flood.

PROVERBS 27:4 NCV

In many ways Alexander the Great lived up to his name. Energetic, versatile, and intelligent, he conquered many kingdoms and ruled most of the world of his time. About the only thing he couldn't always defeat, however, was his anger.

One day, one of his best friends and a general in his army got drunk and began to say derogatory things about Alexander. In anger, Alexander grabbed his spear from one of the soldiers and threw it at his friend, not meaning to hit him. But the spear found its mark and killed his friend on the spot. Overcome with guilt, Alexander went into deep depression. He considered himself a cruel murderer and would have taken his own life if some of his men had not stopped him.[1] You can be the ruler of the world and yet not the ruler of your spirit if you can't control your anger.

How do we control this God-given emotion?

Our society is highly charged with anger. Today we have school and workplace shootings, road rage, and many other acts of violence. We may live in the angriest society in history.

The Book of Proverbs offers us some insight to anger.

THE POWER OF ANGER

First, understand the power of anger. Look at Proverbs 27:4 (NCV): "Anger is cruel and destroys like a flood." Anyone who has seen a flood knows what this verse is saying. Floodwaters can literally move tons of concrete or other debris. Similarly, anger can also cause mass destruction.

Psychologist Neil Clark Warren defines anger as a "physical state of readiness." When we are angry, we prepare to act whether it is in response to hurt, frustration, or fear. Our bodies release sugar into the bloodstream, adrenaline begins to flow, the heart rate and blood pressure rise, and even our eyes dilate so we can see better.[2] We're stronger and more powerful. God gave us the emotion of anger to protect ourselves. When we're angry, our body readies itself for defensive or offensive measures.

Do you remember the Incredible Hulk? Whenever the man got angry, the Hulk in him came out. The angrier he got, the more powerful the Hulk would become. That's a good illustration of anger even in the rest of us who have no "super powers."

Often anger is a response to hurt. For example, at work, you may be next in line for a big promotion. Then the boss gives it to his good friend who is not nearly as qualified as you. That makes you angry.

Maybe you've been criticized by the person you love the most. It hurts. Or maybe you've had a great loss; someone dear to you died. It's not uncommon to become very angry, even with God.

Some years ago a young man was killed in a hunting accident. His girlfriend was extremely angry. She railed at God and then became angry at me because I represented God. She told me she didn't want me to say anything about God at the funeral. If her eyes had been daggers, I would have been dead. As I stood and tried to convey some comfort to the family during the funeral, she stared at me coldly. When we were finished at the cemetery, she refused to leave. So I stayed for awhile and just visited with her until she began to talk.

"I don't know why I'm acting this way; I'm so sorry," she finally said. I told her that her actions were understandable. She was deeply hurt, and that caused great anger in her.

Neil Clark Warren also wrote that anger is a response to frustration. Things don't go the way you want in a situation. A great example is a traffic jam. If you're blocked in traffic, do you just sit back and say, "Well, this is wonderful. I kind of needed a break anyway. I think I'll just rest." If we're honest, we probably feel some sort of anxiety or frustration creeping up the back of our necks.

Or maybe you are great in the car, but you get a new toy for your child, and you're trying to put it together. The directions are all in foreign languages, and things just aren't going well. What's your response to that frustration? Throw the toy out the window?

Or perhaps it's a bad hair day. Or money falls short of the bills, or your health isn't what it should be. Many different things frustrate people, and these things can all lead to unending anger.

Even our biblical heroes got frustrated. Moses frequently got frustrated with the children of Israel. While Moses was on the mountain with God receiving the Law for the people to follow, God reported what was happening in the camp. When Moses returned, he saw that the Israelites had fashioned an idol and were dancing around it, worshiping it instead of God. In anger, Moses threw down the tablets of Law, breaking them.

Fear also leads to anger for many people. We could be threatened somehow. Peter is a good example of this. In Matthew 26, Judas betrayed Jesus, and the soldiers arrested Him. Responding to fear, Peter angrily whipped out his sword and sliced off a person's ear.

Sometimes abused animals lash out and bite because of fear. Some people, afraid of being hurt again, can also lash out unpredictably.

We see from these examples that anger is often a response to some experience in our lives. Is it always negative? No. Its power is neither good nor bad. Anger can be used for constructive as well as destructive purposes.

In fact, as we looked at earlier, the Bible even allows us to be angry. Ephesians 4:26 (NASB) says, "Be angry, and yet do not sin." At times in life, we *should* be angry. Jesus demonstrated that in Matthew 21 when He arrived at the temple during the Passover Feast. Possibly two or three million people traveled to Jerusalem to worship in the temple for this feast. While they were in Jerusalem, the travelers had to pay their temple tax. The people came from different regions and used different kinds of money, but the leaders of the Jews had set up their own system. The temple tax could only be paid with Jewish money. To make it convenient for the people (and to get great profit for themselves), money changers were set up in the temple so the people could exchange their money for Jewish money. These money changers charged exorbitant service fees and cheated the people.

Jesus was angry that the money changers were taking advantage of the people who wanted to worship God in the temple. In righteous anger, Jesus drove out the money changers with a whip. He demonstrated in that moment that anger is a God-given emotion that can be used for good. Was anger about such treatment of people an appropriate and godly response here? I think so.

TAMING THE WILD BEAST

The second insight Proverbs gives us is that we must always control our anger. This is a challenge. Look at Proverbs 16:32 (NCV): "Controlling your temper is better than capturing a city." Capturing a city would be a great feat for anyone, but who can do that? Controlling your anger, though, is for everyone, and Solomon says it's even greater than world conquest.

How then do we learn to control our anger?

Maintain a proper attitude toward yourself. Self-esteem and a proper attitude have much to do with anger. Dr. Les Carter says the way a person handles anger is ultimately a reflection of his or her self-image. People who have poor self-images generally have a problem with anger.

We talked about this in the previous chapter, but let me amplify it. Healthy self-esteem insulates us against the insults and criticism that all of us will face in life. A person with a good self-image can let nasty comments roll off his or her back. But when you struggle with a low self-esteem, those same comments can cut you to the core. Your natural reaction is to respond in defensive anger. Keeping a right perspective of who we are in Christ can go a long way in helping us learn to control our anger.[3]

Don't bottle your anger. Admit when you're angry. Again we find in Ephesians 4:26 (NASB) that you're not to "let the sun go down on your anger." In other words, don't bottle up your anger and carry it around. Don't bury anger on the inside because it will ultimately bury you. It's easy to deny that you're angry. But if you deny that anger, it will turn into bitterness and then into depression. Not all depression is a result of anger, but all unprocessed anger will become depression.

Make a practice of humbly going to the person you have angry feelings toward and working it out. The person may not even realize he or she has angered you. Don't let anger eat at you. Deal with it before the sun sets.

Passive-aggressive anger is another form of anger that looks so cool on the outside. For instance, an advertisement on television shows how passive-aggressive anger works. A truck driver stops at a truck stop, and he's sitting at the counter having a hamburger, fries, and coffee. Three motorcycle gang members walk in with their black leather jackets on and their big hog motorcycles sitting out front.

Wanting to pick a fight, one of them grabs the guy's hamburger and takes a bite out of it. Another one picks up some fries and starts eating them, while the last one drinks the poor guy's coffee. The truck driver, though, stays cool, calm, and collected, pays his bill, and walks out. The motorcycle gang is disappointed because they wanted a fight. One of them tells the waitress, "Not much of a man, is he?" She answers, "I don't know about that, but he's not a very good truck driver, because he just ran over three motorcycles on his way out."

That is passive-aggressive anger in action.

Admit when you're angry and express it. Proverbs 29:11 (NIV) says, "A fool gives full vent to his anger, but a wise man keeps himself under control." Some psychologists say the way to deal with anger is to vent it; go bang your head on the wall or beat on a pillow or something like that. Unfortunately for such strategies, Neil Clark Warren says that anger expressed aggressively may actually make you become even more aggressive.[4]

You can find many nonverbal ways to vent anger. Sometimes we show anger with such actions as a stern look, slamming the door, breaking down and crying, or glaring at someone. These are not the best ways to deal with your anger. Instead, tell the person you are angry with in a very controlled way what he or she has done. Confront him or her gently but firmly. State your case. Then see what the person does with it.

I have had to learn to do that. For a long time I thought it was wrong to say I was angry. So I'd just say I was "a little frustrated." It was really a way of dodging the truth. I had to learn to say, "I want you to know what you are doing makes me very angry."

You might also ask yourself why you want to express that anger. Is it because you're vindictive, or do you want to help this person learn to behave? If your true desire is to help the person, then perhaps your anger is justified and can be used for a good purpose.

LET GO

The third thing Proverbs advises us to learn about anger is to learn to release your anger when it will not lead to good results.

Proverbs 29:8 (NIV) says, "Mockers stir up a city, but wise men turn away anger." Wise men turn away from their anger when they see things are spinning out of control or a worse situation will occur. Sometimes you must just release the anger. Let it go. Forget the whole situation and go about your business.

Don't confuse releasing your anger with suppressing it. Suppressing anger, stuffing it inside, ultimately leads to depression. You release your anger when you see that being angry won't help anyone, so you just let it go.

I had been preaching some messages on anger at church, and one night my son Timothy walked out of the house, slamming the door. I asked him what was wrong, and he said, "I'm just practicing what you're preaching on anger at church by processing my anger!" It was funny, but it did help us work through the problem amicably.

In the same way, my wife, when she served as a principal, learned to let people vent their anger at her. When they finally simmered down, she would earnestly tell them, "I'm glad you could get this out, but please don't talk to me like that again." It often calmed people down.

IT'S A MAD, MAD WORLD

Proverbs also teaches us to learn to be wise in dealing with angry people.

We live in what has been called "The Age of Rage." According to the FBI estimates, a violent crime is committed in the United States every twenty seconds. More than two million women will be battered by their husbands this year, and many men will be battered by their wives. We encounter this "Age of Rage" on highways when drivers literally stop their cars, grab a gun, and shoot the person who cut them off. We encounter it in the marketplace and at school, when young people lose control and shoot up the building. We encounter it at home and, yes, sometimes even at church when meetings become mired in arguments and wrangling.

Solomon says in Proverbs 22:24 (NIV): "Do not make friends with a hot-tempered man, do not associate with one easily angered." Why does he caution us to be careful around angry people? They're like porcupines. You can't get close to them because they have a tendency to fire darts into your face!

Nonetheless, we can't just ignore them, so the question becomes: How do we wisely handle angry people? You may have an angry person in your office. You may be facing an angry neighbor. Or you may have someone angry in your own household: a teen, or a wife, or a mother-in-law.

What do you do?

For one thing, don't retaliate. Jesus said in Matthew 5:38–39 (NCV): "You have heard that it was said, 'An eye for an eye, and a tooth for a tooth.' But I tell you, don't stand up against an evil person. If someone slaps you on the right cheek, turn to him the other cheek also."

If someone slaps you on the right cheek, what are you supposed to do? Slap them back twice as hard? That's what you want to do, isn't it? But Jesus counsels us, "No, just turn the other cheek." It's like a dog deciding not to fight a skunk. He might be able to win, but it's not worth the stink, so he just goes his own way. Don't retaliate.

A man came to our church who had a filthy mouth and would often retaliate against people when he was angry. As he began to grow in the Lord, the way he related to people began to change. His language changed. He became much kinder and emerged as a man who could control himself against even the harshest criticisms and attacks.

A second way to handle angry people is to give a gentle response. Proverbs 15:1 (NIV) tells us, "A gentle answer turns away wrath, but a harsh word stirs up anger." One strategy that helps me in dealing with an angry person is to search for one thing on which to agree. Stress that point, and often the anger is defused.

A third tactic is to think before you act. Psalm 4:4 (NCV) says, "When you are angry, do not sin."

Many years ago Thomas Jefferson said, "When you're angry, count to ten. When you're really angry, count to a hundred." That's a lot better than what Mark Twain said: "Count to four, and then if you're really angry, swear."

The most practical thing to do when handling anger is to learn to love as Jesus does. Study Jesus Christ, and let Him teach you how to respond in a loving way to angry people.

Love isn't always a warm fuzzy feeling, just as forgiveness is never something we feel like doing; rather, it has to be a decision we make, regardless of how we feel.

In the early days of my ministry, we had a meeting about our first building project. No one took the meeting very seriously, and the project wasn't even considered. I went home feeling rejected and very angry. I had to back up and consider my love for the people at that point. I had been there for only a short time, and I didn't really know the people very well. It took twelve months for my love to grow and that vision to form. But as both of those did grow, I learned to lead much better, and the motion for the building project was passed.

Take a moment to reflect on your own level of anger. Do you have a problem with anger, or are you in denial about it? Remember: Harboring anger leads to bitterness and ultimately depression. If we're honest and ask God to change our angry spirits into spirits of love and self-control, He will honor that request. It may take time and effort and prayer, but with God's help, anyone can learn to deal with anger effectively and finally.

CHAPTER 10

WHOM CAN YOU TRUST?

The Proverbs' Teaching on Trust

Trust in the LORD with all your heart.

People who believe anything are called gullible. Most of us have been gullible at some time or another. Some years ago, I owned a Volkswagen Beetle that needed some repairs. I trusted a certain guy to fix it, and boy, did he ever clean out my checkbook! I was gullible.

Then there was a real estate investment that cost me every penny I put into it.

When I was in high school, I trusted my intuitive wisdom when I had a sore throat. I thought drinking something hot was the thing to do, so I drank hot chocolate made with raw milk. I ended up with rheumatic fever.

Americans believe a lot of strange things these days. Some believe Elvis Presley is still living. Many believe in reincarnation of some sort, others believe in ghosts, and still others believe that aliens have visited this planet. Trusting is a vital part of our lives, but we must be careful of what we trust.

When I was a kid, we used to swing on grapevines. These

long, thick vines hung down through a tree, and we would cut the vine off at the bottom. If we found one that leaned out over a hollow, we could swing out twenty to thirty feet from the tree. We'd test it first, swinging on it carefully until we knew we could trust it. One time, a friend of mine shot way out on a grapevine over a depression and it broke. He lay in a body cast from the waist down for the rest of the summer. We put our trust in that grapevine for a long time, but then it crashed on us.

People put their trust in jobs, the stock market, and relationships—only to later have them crash.

According to the Book of Proverbs, wisdom is an indispensable part of trust. Without wisdom, we might trust in the wrong things with devastating results in our lives.

Let's look at what Proverbs teaches about trust.

PUT YOUR WEIGHT ON IT

First, Proverbs 3:5 (NIV) says, "Trust in the LORD with all your heart." What does this mean? The word *trust* means *to rely upon*, *to put all of your weight on*, and *to be confident in*. In essence, trust is risky. When you place your confidence in God, though, you have trusted Someone who won't let you down.

Let me tell you about Dudley. When Dudley turned seventy-five years old, a pilot friend offered to give him a little cruise over the town in his airplane. So Dudley went and flew over the little town. When they landed at the airport, one of Dudley's friends asked, "Dudley, were you afraid?"

Dudley said a little hesitantly, "No, not really, but I never did put all my weight down."[1] Trust is putting all of your weight down.

Trust involves much more than just believing that God exists. Most people in America believe that God exists. Many believe that Jesus Christ really came and died on the cross and did rise out of that tomb. But people can believe all those things, and it still may not change their lives. You can believe in Jesus in your head and still not trust Him for your life.

This verse in Proverbs says to "trust in the LORD with all your heart." That kind of trust can be illustrated by a parachute—a wonderful invention that lets a person float down out of the sky to land without being injured. People who skydive trust their parachutes. Now I believe in parachutes—I've seen people use them and succeed. But have I ever trusted one myself, putting it on, leaping out of an airplane, pulling the rip cord, and landing safely? No, I haven't. Do I plan to trust one like that? No, I don't.

You can't really trust in a parachute in the biblical sense of trust until you jump out of a plane with one strapped to your back. There's a difference in saying you believe in God and truly trusting Him or putting all of your weight on Him.

RELEASING THE POWER

Why is trusting God so important to your life? First of all, trust is the most important ingredient in any relationship. Our relationships can be measured by trust. God longs to have a relationship with us built on trust. He longs that we trust Him with everything—our lives now, our lives after death, the lives of those we love—because He alone can manage those things for us.

Trust is also important because it releases the power of the thing that is trusted. Only when we trust God do we see His blessing and power released in our lives.

Again, this can be illustrated with the parachute example. Skydivers release the potential of parachutes by pulling the rip cord and floating down out of the sky. Until then, the parachute is just a limp rag in a sack. But when we trust ourselves to the parachute, letting it hold us up as we plummet down through the sky, we see its true power.

In the same way, when we trust God, we release His potential to work in our lives. Trust in God releases the power of Jesus Christ to save us and transform us. It releases His redemptive work in our lives. Like John 1:12 (NIV) says, "To those who believed in his name, he gave the right [or the power] to become children of God." The reason why this trusting business is so important is because it's the only way a person can have a loving relationship with God.

Trust tends to be fairly easy when everything goes all right in our lives. However, James Dobson says in his book *When God Doesn't Make Sense,* "Faith never goes unchallenged for long."[2] Sooner or later, you're going to hit a bump in the road that will send you careening through the air with no set-down in sight. That's when trust comes into play. It will happen to all of us.

But what happens then? When things turn sour on us, we tend to ask, "Where is God?" We want to know why God doesn't do something about our situation. Dobson goes on to say, "Apparently most believers are permitted to go through emotional and spiritual valleys that are designed to test their faith in the crucible of fire. Why? Because faith ranks at the top of God's system of priorities."[3] God builds trust through putting us into situations where we have to trust Him. That's the only way we can achieve it.

Perhaps you are in the middle of some tremendous tests in your life. Don't despair. God is training you. He is building your level of trust in Him. He is teaching you to trust Him even when everything looks wrong. When we have faith in God even though our lives are topsy-turvy, that's true trust. Any other brand simply doesn't cut it. I don't know of any great people who have not gone through tremendous trials. It is part of the process of exercising trust in God.

I never did like tests in school, but they stretched me academically. I particularly disliked pop quizzes. You never knew when they were coming, so you just had to study every day. The teacher smiled, told us to pull out our pencils, and life went haywire for the next five minutes.

Like school, life is full of pop quizzes. They are not meant to destroy us, but to stretch us a little.

WHERE ARE YOU LEANING?

The second part of Proverbs 3:5 (NIV) is to "Lean not on your own understanding." *Lean not* is the opposite of faith. The writer of Proverbs is saying, "Don't depend on your own understanding." We need to know our limitations in our own mental and psychological comprehension of a situation or event.

I once read an article entitled "178 Seconds to Live." It was about twenty pilots training on flight simulators. These pilots had a lot of experience flying by sight, but they had not been trained using the instrument panel of an airplane. Each pilot was placed in a flight simulator and had to completely trust on instruments and not his own instincts. Interestingly, the pilots lasted an average of 178 seconds before they crashed. When they used their own instincts—their own understanding of the situation—and failed to rely on the instrument panel, every one of them crashed.[4] Similarly, God wants us to use our minds, but frequently our own understanding isn't enough.

God uses a word in the Bible to describe the result of leaning on our own understanding: *pride.* How do we guard ourselves against it? Number one is to make knowing God a top priority. Proverbs 2:6 (NIV) says, "For the LORD gives wisdom, and from his mouth come knowledge and understanding."

What is the Bible about? Wisdom, knowledge, and understanding about God. Trusting God does not mean you don't think on your own. Rather, as we use our minds, we need to gain a proper view of God. Otherwise, our decisions will be distorted.

A good example of this occurred in the Garden of Eden (Genesis 3). As Satan tempted Eve to eat the fruit of the Tree of the Knowledge of Good and Evil, he said, "You will not surely die. . .for God knows that when you eat of it your eyes will be opened, and you will be like God, knowing good and evil" (Genesis 3:4–5 NIV). What had Satan done? He cast doubt about God's character. As a result, Eve doubted that God truly had her best in mind by asking her to not eat it.

When we doubt God's character, it destroys everything we know about God's power in our lives. On the other hand, the more we understand about God's true character, the more we can trust Him.

Leaning not on your understanding also means being open to the advice of godly people. Proverbs 12:15 (NIV) says, "The way of a fool seems right to him, but a wise man listens to advice." Get some good godly people around you. Listen to their counsel and trust their advice when they give it.

When I was a kid, polio was a dreaded disease. I remember some kids who heard that if you drank Purex, a laundry product, you wouldn't get polio. Well, you probably wouldn't because you'd be dead. They may have been right, but I took one whiff of that stuff and decided against their counsel.

Plenty of people will offer advice on any subject. Sometimes their advice may be bad, like the boys and the Purex, or good. To guarantee your chances of good advice, find godly people who can provide godly counsel. Every major decision in our church is a group effort. I rely on the wise people around me to help me make big decisions. I know I cannot poll the church audience, but I will seek help from people who have knowledge about a specific issue and can give good input.

If you want to guard against leaning on your own understanding, make your plans, but don't leave God out of them. Proverbs talks a lot about such planning. Proverbs 21:5 (NIV) says, "The plans of the diligent lead to profit." Proverbs 16:9 (NASB) says, "The mind of man plans his way, but the LORD directs his steps." It's marvelous to make plans with God directing you. Watching how He works such things out is a pleasure and also a source of encouragement in our Christian walk.

One day in the church where I first worked as a pastor, I talked to a group of people about sermon planning. One lady asked, quite sincerely, "What do you mean, sermon planning?"

I told her I blocked out time each week to prepare my sermon. She was astonished. "I thought you just got up there," she said, "and God filled your mouth."

I wish it were that easy, but I also know that God works through the planning process.

Every person on our staff writes out a ministry plan each year. Occasionally, we go through a strategic planning process for our church. It is irresponsible to say, "I am trusting God," and not make plans. The key is to lean on the understanding that comes from God *as* we plan. To lean on your own understanding without God's input can be disastrous.

STEPS OF FAITH

How, then, do you grow in this business of trusting the Lord? Proverbs 3:5 (NIV) tells us to trust the Lord with all of our hearts and not lean on our own understanding. Proverbs 3:6 continues, "In all your ways acknowledge him, and he will make your paths straight."

Take a look first at the meaning of the word *acknowledge*. The Hebrew word here is found in the Old Testament more than a thousand times. In Proverbs the word *acknowledge* is mentioned thirty-three times. We find it in Genesis 4:1 (NKJV): "Now Adam knew Eve his wife, and she conceived and bore Cain." Adam knew (or acknowledged) Eve by much more than a name; he knew her intimately and sexually. When the Bible talks about *acknowledging*, it's talking about a knowledge that is deep, intimate, and personal.

I remember my first speedboat ride. We traveled to Rockaway Beach quite a bit when I was a kid, and I often hung around on the boat dock. One day, one of our friends, Charlie, a speedboat driver, had a place for one more rider. Charlie told me to jump in. I was excited until he took off. That boat went every way but the way I thought it should, and I thought my life was over. I found myself sitting in the bottom of the boat, frightened, with Charlie looking like he had just arrived at Disney World.

Scrunched up on that floor, I soon began to think. Charlie was a good family friend. I'd known him all my life. Therefore, I began to feel I could trust him. Before the boat ride ended, I was up in my seat yelling and having fun with everyone else. It wasn't because I had so much courage, but because I knew Charlie.

When you know God personally, life can bank to the right and the left; it can look stormy and terrible, but you have confidence that everything will ultimately be okay. It happens because you can stop and think, *I know Jesus; He's my friend. He's been my friend for a long time, and I can trust Him.*

You get to know God better by spending time with Him. So the question is: Are you spending good, quality time with Jesus every day, praying, and reading His Word? That's acknowledging Him in all you do.

Sometime ago a youth group in Holland, Michigan, read *In His Steps*. You've probably heard of the book—it was a bestseller in the early twentieth century and has sold widely since. The students decided to apply the story's teaching by asking a certain question every time they needed to make a decision. They thought this would make a difference in their lives and in the world. What was the question? "What would Jesus do?" WWJD. That's acknowledging Him in all that you do. When you recognize Jesus' presence and interest in your life, you act differently. When that personal relationship becomes vivid in your mind, you trust Him with all that you are.

To the "acknowledge" clause, Proverbs 3:6 (NIV) adds, "He will make your paths straight." Another way to say it is that "He will direct your path." He will show you the path to take. Sometimes God will show us a path that makes sense and looks easy. Other times, the path He points to will not be very appealing. It looks difficult and rough and will take courage to walk.

I see an illustration of this from the lives of Abraham and Lot. The flocks of Abraham and Lot grew so large that the fields weren't large enough. So Abraham and Lot decided to split up and each go a different direction. Abraham let Lot choose which direction he wanted to go. Lot chose the most appealing way, the Jordan Valley where the grass was green, lush, and well watered. Eventually, that road took him to two cities of that lush plain called Sodom and Gomorrah. You probably know what happened there.

The most appealing, easy, and inviting path is not always the wisest path to take. Abraham went in another direction, where the ground was drier and less productive, but it was the wiser path. God revealed His plan to Abraham one step at a time, but it was the path that led to survival and blessing.

Seeing Far Enough to Keep Going

My wife once spoke to a women's meeting near Oklahoma. The morning we got up to travel to the meeting, it was so foggy I could hardly see the road. But while the fog was bad, we could still see far enough ahead of our car to make the trip. We arrived without any problems. Why? I could see some of the way down the road—not far, but far enough to be safe. When I reached the part I had seen, guess what? I could now see the next bit, not much farther, but far enough to keep driving. As I drove, the fog remained hovering over the road, but I could always see just far enough to keep going.

Is your life foggy? What do you do? If God is showing you just one step, take it. Don't wait for Him to show you the whole way; He may never do that. If you take the step He is showing you, He'll show you the next step and the next. You can't see very far, but you have faith that God has seen the end He's taking you to, and that's enough. You can trust Him to get you there.

It may be foggy where you're living right now, too. You may feel confused and disoriented because you don't understand so many things. But if God shows you enough of the road to get going, maybe just one step, my word for you is, take it!

That step could be in any area of your life—spiritually, your church, your workplace, a relationship, or facet of family life. God may want you to change jobs or just change your attitude toward your spouse. He may be tugging at your heart to volunteer at church in some area. You don't see how it will all work out, but He is whispering for you to trust Him with that first step. When we fully trust in Him and follow Him with all our hearts, we can count on Him to make our paths straight and reveal to us the next step.

For some people who are reading these words, that first step may be to trust Christ as Savior. You may be trying to figure out if you can really live the Christian life before taking that step. But I say, trust God enough to take that one step. You will find that the next part of the road will be visible once you take it.

For others, the next step could be obeying in a certain area of your life or being willing to serve others in ministry. Whatever your issue is, Solomon has a bit of wisdom for you: Trust the Lord with all your heart and don't lean on your own understanding. In all your ways acknowledge Him, and He will make your paths straight.

CHAPTER 11

WORK

THAT KEEPS YOU COMING BACK

Finding Joy in Your Job

Hard work brings prosperity.

PROVERBS 28:19 TLB

How do you feel about work?

Some time ago a man told me he disliked his job so much he gets ill every Sunday afternoon to the point of vomiting. Another man told me that many times he would drive up to the parking lot at work, sit there for a moment, and then go home and call in sick. In contrast, some people are like Thomas Edison, who said he never worked a day his life because it was all fun. Which best represents your attitude toward your work? Is it great? Or is it punishment?

Working is a major part of life. If work is not fulfilling, then you're wasting a lot of life. How do you make work something that is meaningful and rewarding? Proverbs gives us some lessons about how to be wise with our work.

OFF TO WORK WE GO

The first principle in Proverbs is to be diligent in your work. Why? Because it brings great profit. Look at some of the following verses. Proverbs 28:19 (TLB): "Hard work brings prosperity." Proverbs 14:23 (NIV): "All hard work brings a profit." Proverbs 12:24 (NIV): "Diligent hands will rule." Proverbs 10:4 (NIV): "Diligent hands bring wealth." And Proverbs 21:5 (NIV): "The plans of the diligent lead to profit."

That sampling of verses confirms that profit in life comes from working diligently. What exactly did Solomon mean by *diligent* work? The word translated as *diligently* is sometimes also translated as *sharp*. *Sharp* means that your focus is placed on that one spot; all the leverage is directed at one point. When we say *diligence* can be described as being *sharp*, it means we focus our energies and give it all we've got.

How do you work diligently? The key is attitude—how you perceive work. For example, one way to look at work is that it's a necessary evil, something bad, or simply something that has to be done. As long as you look at work in a negative light, your energies will be drained. When you're working—whether it's your homework, chores around the home, or being employed in the marketplace—check your thought processes. In the back of your mind are you saying, *I have to. I need to. I ought to. I should?* If those kinds of thoughts go through your mind as you work, you will be drained emotionally and physically.

On the flip side, if you look at work as something positive, it will energize you. For example, as a child, I had several chores around the house that I viewed negatively. I'd feel tired just thinking about them, and I'd say to my folks, "I think I'm too tired to do this." But if somebody came along and said, "Let's go play basketball," I would instantly receive a miraculous surge of energy. My energies slackened because of my attitude toward those chores. We all have the choice to let our work be a drain or an energy source, depending on which way we view it.

There's a caution here: Be diligent, but don't become a workaholic. Proverbs 23:4 (NIV) says, "Do not wear yourself out to get rich; have the wisdom to show restraint." A companion verse is in Ecclesiastes 10:15 (TEV): "Only someone too stupid to find his way home would wear himself out with work."

Are you a workaholic? Before you answer too quickly, maybe you should ask your spouse or a close friend. Many people don't recognize they're acting like workaholics. Was Thomas Edison a workaholic? I don't think so. There is a big difference between being driven compulsively in your work and being passionate about your work. The workaholic's compulsive drive to work usually comes from some need on the inside, such as acceptance. Somehow the satisfaction of working makes the person feel more acceptable to the people around him or her. On the other hand, passion about work energizes us in a positive way. Which are you? Do you go to work hating it, or do you have a passion that says, "I *get* to do this now"?

LIGHTENING THE WORKAHOLIC LOAD

Just in case you are a workaholic, here are several ways to deal more effectively with that drive. First, find security in God's love. Consider 1 John 3:1 (NLT): "See how very much our heavenly Father loves us, for he allows us to be called his children, and we really are!" Do you feel totally secure in God's care? Or do you feel that you have to earn someone else's love and care? Do you feel that if you work a little bit more, people or God will think better of you?

Second, learn to enjoy what you have. The Ecclesiastes writer says all of us should eat and drink and enjoy what we have worked for. Are you content in what you have, or do you think that just a little bit more would make you happier?

Third, faithfully practice a day of rest. I've struggled with this one. I know the proverb says, "A relaxed attitude lengthens life" (Proverbs 14:30 NLT). However, a number of years ago, I had to force myself to take off a day from work and do something more relaxing. I had so much to do around the church, so much planning, and so many important meetings. But I took that day off. At first I fidgeted, wondering what was happening at church. But then I began to remind myself that I needed to relax. It wasn't easy, but eventually it became a time of refreshing and renewing.

Fourth, value what is truly valuable. Mark 8:36 (NIV) says, "What good is it for a man to gain the whole world, yet forfeit his soul?" For years I thought this verse spoke only to unbelievers, telling them, "So what if you gain the whole world and go to hell?" I didn't see that it said anything to Christians. However, it may actually say more to Christians than to unbelievers. The word *forfeit* here means *to damage*. What good is it if you gain the whole world, but you damage your soul, and it goes into heaven undeveloped? What good is it if you have a big bank account but go into heaven a spiritual gnat?

The challenge is to ask the question, "What is really important in life?" If it's our souls, then we need to live in a way that doesn't damage our souls, the part of us that lives forever. Think about working diligently for the Lord. Part of working for the Lord is not overworking and neglecting our souls.

HAVING THE RIGHT REASONS

Proverbs shows us another point: Go to work with the right purpose in mind. What's the purpose of work? Is it just to pay the bills? Is work a sort of punishment? God didn't slap work on us because we sinned. Adam and Eve worked before sin ever came into the world.

I think the main reason we work is pretty obvious: It provides for our needs. First Timothy 5:8 (NIV) says, "If anyone does not provide for his relatives, and especially for his immediate family, he has denied the faith and is worse than an unbeliever." More bluntly, Paul says in 2 Thessalonians 3:10 that anyone who refuses to work should not eat. We know we aren't to be idle, but is there more to work than just paying the bills or financing our greens' fees or extra trips to the mall?

A second reason for work is that it's a way to gain wealth, not only for us, but also for the benefit of others. Thirdly, work develops our skills and character. And fourth, it's a way to serve God and others and also glorify God.

Take a hard look at Proverbs 21:5 (NCV): "The plans of hard-working people earn a profit." Profit is more than paying the bills; it's a way to make it possible to experience some of the great pleasures of life—travel, eating out, gifts for others, and so on.

Remember what Deuteronomy 8:18 (NIV) says about wealth. "But remember the LORD your God, for it is he who gives you the ability to produce wealth." Wealth is simply having a little bit more than you need. So let me ask you, do you have more than you need?

If we are honest, most of us in the United States admit we have more than we need, especially when compared to the rest of the world. Why would God let us have more than we need? Paul tells us in Ephesians 4:28 (NIV): "Doing something useful with his own hands, that he may have something to share with those in need." Paul shows us that we have wealth in order to help others in need.

Look closely at yourself to determine what is a need and what is a want. Our materialistic society with all of its advertising breeds great want in our lives. We want this. We need that. It's an endless circle. Let Jesus be Lord over your finances and purchasing decisions, and you won't be stricken by constant wants based on marketing. That's part of good stewardship.

If you find you have more wealth than you need, I challenge you to take a mission trip in the next few years. Pay for it out of your own wealth. How? If you set aside a little every month for a project like that, in three or five years you could go anyplace in the world you'd like to minister to others. When you give your life away in ministry, you receive rewards not only in heaven but also here on earth. When you see the delight on the faces of the people you help, when you hear their thanks and their praises to God for what you have done, your spirit will be filled to overflowing. One of the best investments you can ever make in life is to give your life away to others. God will let you have wealth not so you can die with a big bank account, but so you can in some way meet someone else's needs.

WORKING FOR SKILLS

Work also helps us develop our skills. Ecclesiastes 10:10 (NIV) says, "If the ax is dull and its edge unsharpened, more strength is needed but skill will bring success." Where do you get skill? Do you develop skill by reading a textbook? Do you develop skill by sitting in a seminar or by going to a class? Maybe a little. But we really develop skill on the job. My skill to preach didn't come out of a textbook. I didn't listen to a tape. I worked at it. You cannot imagine how pitiful I was in those early days of preaching.

We usually respect someone who has a great skill. If you needed heart bypass surgery and you got to choose between someone who made top grades in the country's finest medical school and someone who's been performing these surgeries for a few years, whom would you pick? I would prefer the surgeon who has developed his or her skill through experience. Work, time, practice, and patience develop skill.

Work also builds our character. Paul speaks of character as he describes the fruit of the Spirit in Galatians 5:22–23 (NIV): "But the fruit of the Spirit is love, joy, peace, patience, kindness, goodness, faithfulness, gentleness and self-control." How do we get the fruit of the Spirit in our lives? By working at it. God gives us wonderful opportunities to grow in patience, perhaps by having to work with a challenging coworker or boss. You may grow in gentleness by having a rough-and-ready child or by caring for an aging parent. God often builds character as we work through difficult circumstances.

God built my character so that I had to learn how to handle stress. Back in the early '80s, we had a building project going that required us to borrow money at 16 percent interest. I had not learned how to manage my thinking processes at that time, so I had a lot of junky thinking going on in my head. It drained my energy. That turned out to be a great learning experience as I discovered how to manage stressful situations by managing my thinking processes. That's when I first learned that stress is in your head, how you think about the circumstances rather than the circumstances themselves. We ended up borrowing the money, building the church, and all turned out well.

WORK AS A SERVICE

Work is also a way to serve God and others. Colossians 3:23 (NIV) says, "Whatever you do, work at it with all your heart, as working for the Lord, not for men." We don't work just for profit or for our families or ourselves; no, we work for the Lord. When you go to a job or to school or even as you do the chores around the house, don't think, *Ugh, I have to get this done now!*

No, you say, "I'm doing this for God." Paul went on to say in the next verse of Colossians 3 (NIV): "You know that you will receive an inheritance from the Lord as a reward." You may get a paycheck at the end of the week, but the greatest reward is waiting for you in heaven.

Lastly, work is a way to honor and glorify God. Jesus said in Matthew 5:16 (NIV): "Let your light shine before men, that they may see your good deeds and praise your Father in heaven." Many of you share your faith at work and invite friends and others to come to your church. If you have tried to honor God, when you invite these people to church, they might say "yes" because of what they have seen in you.

I have found that many people come to church because of the godly and loving attitudes of another Christian. It's also true that many people do not go to church because of what they have seen in the life of another Christian. If we go to work and announce that we're Christians, but our lives and work contradict what we say, we will have a negative impact on our coworkers and their view of Christ. But when we see our work as a way to glorify God, we have a positive impact on the people around us for Christ.

INTEGRITY IN WORK

Also, work with unquestionable integrity. Integrity means *complete* or *undivided* or *the same through and through*.

If you have ever visited Universal Studios, you know that many magnificent-looking houses line the street. However, when you open the front door, you don't find a living room, kitchen, or other living space. It's a mock-up, made simply for show.

That's not integrity. A person who looks one way on the outside but is quite different on the inside will not make a mark for Christ. I have met people who exhibit what I call compartmentalized integrity. They have high-quality integrity in one area of their lives, but they exhibit big flaws in other areas of their lives. That's a danger to them and others. It will drive people away from them and from Christ.

Here's a true example. Some time ago in Riverside, California, a man and woman went on a picnic. They stopped to purchase some food at a fast food chicken restaurant. Instead of getting chicken, however, they were given a box full of the cash received by the restaurant so far that day. The manager of the store always took the money to the bank in a chicken box so no one would know money was inside.

When the couple reached their lakeside retreat and opened the box, they found a bigger picnic than they had planned for! Nonetheless, they were people of integrity, so they took the box back to the manager. The manager wanted to call the newspapers and tell them about this great act of honesty. The man, however, refused. His integrity only went so far, and he admitted that the woman he was with was not his wife.

Isn't it interesting that he had such admirable integrity in one area of his life and such failure in another?

Integrity is when we open the door and look inside and find the same quality there as we do on the outside. Is that you? Do you have as much integrity in your work when no one else is looking as when they are? Solomon says that integrity pays well. Whether people are looking or not, integrity reaps tremendous dividends in life.

This is verified in Proverbs 10:9 (NIV): "The man of integrity walks securely." In other words, the man of integrity doesn't have to worry about covering his tracks. Proverbs 11:3 (NIV) adds, "The integrity of the upright guides them." If you have integrity, you will always know what to do in any given situation. No confusion. No dire prayers into the night. Your integrity guides you into all truth.

Proverbs 2:6–7 (NASB) says, "For the LORD gives wisdom; from His mouth come knowledge and understanding. He stores up sound wisdom for the upright; He is a shield to those who walk in integrity." When it says, "He is a shield to those who walk in integrity," does that mean God will shield you from bad things in life? No. It means God will shield you from making dumb mistakes. God will give you wisdom.

In Proverbs 20:7 (NIV) we read, "The righteous man leads a blameless life; blessed are his children after him." Integrity pays well. Integrity is a big thing in my life, but I didn't learn it from a book. I didn't even learn it because my dad drilled it into me. I learned it by watching my dad and mom live before me. They made a tremendous impact on my life. Your children will benefit from your integrity.

So I ask, do your kids have that benefit? Do they see you act with integrity in every business deal? Or do they see that you bring little items home from work that don't belong to you? Do they see you call in sick when you're not really sick? Are you giving them the benefit of watching integrity in action, or are you just trying to tell them about it? The impact comes when they see it modeled day in and day out.

Working with integrity can be tough. It is not always popular. "Bloodthirsty men hate a man of integrity and seek to kill the upright," says Proverbs 29:10 (NIV). When I worked in the secular marketplace, I was often shocked at the pressure to cheat and to lie and to shirk on my work. I found out quickly that trying to walk with integrity wasn't always popular.

Proverbs 28:6 (NASB) says, "Better is the poor who walks in his integrity than he who is crooked though he be rich." Mark that verse down. People around you may have no integrity, and yet it looks like everything's going their way. They seem to get rich even though they have turned their backs on God. On the other hand, you will try to do everything right, yet things don't seem to go your way. How do you put that together?

God talks about such people in Psalm 73:3–20 (NCV). "I was jealous of proud people. I saw wicked people doing well. They are not suffering; they are healthy and strong. They don't have troubles like the rest of us; they don't have problems like other people. They wear pride like a necklace and put on violence as their clothing. They are looking for profits and do not control their selfish desires. They make fun of others and speak evil; proudly they speak of hurting others. They brag to the sky. They say that they own the earth. So their people turn to them and give them whatever they want. They say, 'How can God know?' These people are wicked, always at ease, and getting richer. So why have I kept my heart pure? Why have I kept my hands from doing wrong? I have suffered all day long; I have been punished every morning. God, if I had decided to talk like this, I would have let your people down. I tried to understand all this, but it was too hard for me to see until I went to the Temple of God. Then I understood what will happen to them. You have put them in danger; you cause them to be destroyed. They are destroyed in a moment; they are swept away by terrors. It will be like waking from a dream. Lord, when you rise up, they will disappear."

The psalmist here reveals he doesn't understand why people who lack integrity seem to thrive while he is suffering. But at the temple, God spoke to him, and he began to see that those people were just living in a dream and were in for a rude awakening.

You may be in for a rude awakening. You're cheating, you're doing things dishonestly, and you're doing things you know you should not do. And because the hammer hasn't fallen, you think you will get by with this. But God showed the psalmist that there will be a wake-up day. The bubble will pop. That day may be here on earth, or that time might come on Judgment Day, when Christ, on His throne, judges all of our deeds.

A life full of integrity truly does pay, and if that reward doesn't come in this life, we will receive it in eternity. God always keeps His promises.

CHAPTER 12

SELF-DISCIPLINE

FOR THE UNDISCIPLINED

Get Control of Yourself

Like a city whose walls are broken down
is a man who lacks self-control.

PROVERBS 25:28 NIV

A man took a test for a commercial license to drive an eighteen-wheeler. "You're going down a mountain, and suddenly the brakes go out," they told him. "At the foot of the mountain, a train is crossing the highway. You try to downshift, but the gear is stuck in seventh gear. You hit the emergency brake, but nothing happens. You look for a drive-off, but there is none. What do you do?"

He thought for a moment and then said, "I'd reach back into the sleeper and wake up Ollie."

"Why would you wake Ollie?" the examiner asked.

"Because Ollie's never seen a real bad train and truck wreck like this one's going to be."

If you don't have self-control in life, you'd better wake up Ollie, because you're in for a great wreck. Many careers have been destroyed by the lack of self-control. In fact, the same goes for many marriages. Friendships end up bashed on the rocks because of a lack of self-control. A whole life can be decimated by people who cannot discipline themselves.

The question we need to answer is: How do you gain and maintain self-control?

It's not uncommon for brilliant, talented, beautiful people with great people skills to lack self-control. They sometimes end up making a terrible mess of their lives because of it.

The Book of Proverbs offers us much wisdom on how to gain and grow in self-discipline. Remember, Proverbs was written to a younger generation from their elders to show them how to put life together successfully. It reads like a father giving great advice to a son. But he does not quit before giving that boy some advice about self-control.

In Proverbs 16:32 (NLT), he said, "It is better to be patient than powerful; it is better to have self-control than to conquer a city." That's how important self-control is. Look at Proverbs 25:28 (NIV): "Like a city whose walls are broken down is a man who lacks self-control."

What's the big deal about the walls of the city being broken down? In that day, if a city's walls were broken, it lost its protection from its enemies. It was vulnerable. Without self-control, you are vulnerable just like that city.

I'd like to give you several ways to develop self-control from the Book of Proverbs.

ADMITTING THE NEED

The first step in gaining and maintaining self-control is to admit your need for this quality in your life. Proverbs 13:18 (NIV) says, "He who ignores discipline comes to poverty and shame." Here, the word *ignore* means *to neglect, avoid,* or *be out of control.* If you are avoiding, neglecting, denying, or ignoring the fact that you need self-discipline, you'll probably never find it.

Many people today suffer from addictions—from sex, alcohol, and drug addictions to food and pleasure addictions. The first step to recovery for such people is admitting they need help. In the original twelve-step program for alcoholics developed by Alcoholics Anonymous, the second step calls them to believe that a power greater than themselves can restore them to sanity.

Apply that principle for every person struggling with self-control. First, we admit we need help; then we admit we need God to heal us. Ask yourself some hard questions. Do you have self-control over eating and drinking? Can you stop eating when you're full? Do you only eat when you are truly hungry, or do you have a habit of eating for other reasons?

Second, do you have self-control over spending money? Are you a sucker for bargains or a compulsive buyer?

Do you have control over your sexual desire? Do you abstain from viewing pornography? Are you self-controlled on a date?

Do you have self-control over how you spend your time? Do you find yourself constantly saying, "I don't have enough time to do this; I don't have enough time to do that," and are you always running out of time?

One phrase I say to myself over and over, especially in stressful times, is, "There is enough time for the things that God wants me to do." Do you agree with that statement? It comes down to one of two things: Either I'm doing stuff I shouldn't be doing, or I'm not doing what I should be doing efficiently.

There is always enough time if I have self-discipline.

Here's another question: Do you have control over your anger? Does your temper get the best of you? How about control over your tongue? Or your thoughts? Do you have negative, immoral, or depressive thoughts? These are just a few areas in which we might need a little help with self-control.

Actually, the Book of Proverbs begins by talking about self-control. Proverbs 1:1–2 (NCV) says, "These are the wise words of Solomon son of David, king of Israel. They teach wisdom and self-control; they will help you understand wise words." Will you accept the guidance of Proverbs' wisdom and apply it to your life?

Look at Proverbs 1:7 (NCV): "Knowledge begins with respect for the Lord, but fools hate wisdom and self-control." A fool ignores self-discipline and self-control. The first step in having self-discipline or self-control is to admit your need.

LEARN TO WAIT

The second step to developing self-control is to practice delayed gratification. This is a big one. Every winner of any contest understands delayed gratification. Some of our students at church rehearsed many hours for a music contest. They set aside things they really wanted to do to practice. Several received the top rating and will compete in a state music competition. They are beginning to reap the rewards of delayed gratification.

We can keep two things in mind about delayed gratification. The first is that we must make a decision to pay now and play later. Discipline on the front end of a project is very seldom a joy. Hebrews 12:11 (NIV) says, "No discipline seems pleasant at the time, but painful." Isn't that true? The verse continues, "Later on, however, it produces a harvest of righteousness and peace for those who have been trained by it."

We don't find a lot of enjoyment in studying for an exam, practicing running for a marathon, or even pushing back from the table. Holding your tongue when you'd really like to tell someone what you think is tough. Sticking to your budget can bring great pain. None of this is easy, but it pays great dividends.

Look at Proverbs 10:17 (NIV): "He who heeds discipline shows the way to life." He who studies for exams reaps the rewards of good grades. She who trains for a marathon earns a strong body and maybe even a marathon win. He who is willing to push back from the table reaps great health. She who says no to sex outside of marriage prepares the way to a great relationship in marriage. He who is disciplined in his budget is able to achieve the financial goals he sets. Self-control pays big rewards.

The second thing about practicing delayed gratification is to learn to set goals to win. Goals require measurable steps of delayed gratification. By setting goals—little steps on the way to the big goal—you can achieve what you want little by little.

I remember the first camera I bought. I tried to talk my parents into giving me the money for it, but they wouldn't budge. They said if I wanted a camera, I could save my money and buy it. So I set a goal to buy a camera. Every now and then I made some extra money, though, and I'd have to decide whether to save it for the camera or spend it. Practicing delayed gratification and saving my money eventually brought me great joy as a kid when that camera became one of my most prized possessions.

We find tremendous joy in setting goals and keeping on

target. The apostle Paul understood that. In fact, he talked about setting goals in 1 Corinthians 9:25–27 (NCV): "All those who compete in the games use self-control. . .so I do not run without a goal. I fight like a boxer who is hitting something— not just the air. I treat my body hard and make it my slave so that I myself will not be disqualified after I have preached to others." Paul set goals and beat his body into shape so he could make sure he won in the work of the ministry.

DECIDE AHEAD OF TIME

Here's a third way to develop self-control: Decide to do or not do some things in advance, before a situation arises. I see at least four decisions you can make now, well ahead of time, that will help you on your way to self-discipline. The first is to decide to live by a well-thought-out plan. Proverbs 14:22 (NIV) says, "But those who plan what is good find love and faithfulness." In other words, plan how you use your time. Take some time at the close of each day, and write down on a three-by-five card what you will do the next day hour by hour. The next morning, pick it up and follow it. Stick with your plan. You'll have enough time to do everything God wants you to do.

A second area of planning is budgeting your spending. Even before you earn your income, plan how you will spend it, and stick with your plan.

The same is true for exercising self-control in eating. Have a plan and stick with it. If you write down in advance what you will eat each day, it will be a lot easier to hang in there when the desire for excess food strikes.

The second decision you can make ahead of time is to decide to stay away from whatever tempts you. Proverbs 5:8 (NIV) says, "Keep to a path far from her, do not go near the door of her house." What is he talking about? The father is saying, "Watch out, son, because you cannot handle sexual temptation. Stay away from a temptress's house." If you are weak in an area, don't put yourself in a vulnerable position. Go the other direction.

Paul talked about this in 2 Timothy 2:22 (NASB): "Flee from youthful lusts and pursue righteousness." Don't try and stand up to it. Don't stand around waiting for inspiration or a miracle. No—flee. Most of us can stand up to many come-ons, but not against sexual temptations from a skilled tempter.

Our student choir recently performed a musical called, "True Love Waits." The musical's lessons focus on standing strong sexually by not putting yourself into tempting situations. Many of our teens have committed to abstain from sex until they are married. To fulfill their pledges, they will have to stay away from sexual temptations, just as the proverb writer says.

Of course, all of us are different, and some things that tempt you won't tempt me and vice versa. Some people are vulnerable to the temptation of alcohol. I can honestly tell you that I am not tempted by alcohol. But put me by a pecan pie, and that's another matter. Some people struggle with lying. Some people battle workaholic tendencies. Decide in advance to stay away from the things that tempt you.

A third powerful decision concerns what you will let your mind dwell on. Proverbs 23:7 (NASB) is a great verse regarding this: "For as he thinks within himself, so he is." The key to self-control is controlling what you think. You may not be able to control your emotions, but you can control your thoughts, and your thoughts drive your behavior.

What do I mean? Although you can't control the thoughts that dash into your mind at a given moment, you can control whether or not they remain in your mind and receive a chance to grow and thrive. You can reject bad thoughts by placing another thought in your mind. It takes practice and discipline, but it is possible to replace negative, immoral, lustful, or evil thoughts with better ones. That's where Scripture memory can come in handy. Nothing knocks out an immoral thought better than a verse from God's Word.

A perfect illustration of controlling thoughts comes from King David's life. Having decided not to go to war, he stood on his balcony and saw Bathsheba. His first thought was probably, *Wow, she's beautiful!*

He should have stopped his thought process there by turning away and perhaps even quoting, "You shall not commit adultery." Instead, though, David said to himself, *I'm not sure if my eyes caught all that,* and he looked again. This time he said, *Wow, wow, she is incredible. I've got to meet her!*

As he continued looking, his thoughts went even further. *Maybe we can have dinner together. I'm not going to do anything, just talk. I might give her a job or something.* Before long he ended up in bed with Bathsheba. David sinned because he didn't put that first thought out of his mind. When you discipline your thinking by dousing it in God's Word, you're well on the road to self-discipline.

Surrender to the Holy Spirit

Fourth, develop self-control by deciding to continually surrender your life to the Holy Spirit. Ephesians 5:18 (NLT) says, "Let the Holy Spirit fill and control you." Self-control is a fruit of the Spirit (Galatians 5:22–23). Self-control is a work of God's Spirit within us. Study the teachings of the Bible on how to have a Spirit-filled life. God's Spirit not only wants to come into our lives; He wants to guide and direct our lives. He wants to help us have self-control.

How does that work? For one thing, if you want the Holy Spirit to fill and control your life, you have to surrender your life to Him. Surrender means to "empty your life" so the Spirit can "fill it back in."

For instance, to fill a milk carton with water, you have to empty the milk. If you're going to fill it with milk, you have to empty out the water. To be filled with the Holy Spirit, you have to empty out your own natural desires, motives, and needs.

The second step is to receive the Holy Spirit in the control center of your life. You may say that sounds like what you did when you became a Christian, and you're right. The principle is the same as that of receiving Christ as your Savior. To receive Jesus Christ as your Savior, you must repent of your sins and turn loose of your sinful nature. By faith, Christ comes into our lives and takes over. He begins to lead and direct us in the way He wants us to go. That's the control of the Spirit.

How do we walk in the fullness of the Holy Spirit? It is a day-by-day process. We continually empty the bad stuff out of our lives, confessing our sins, admitting our need for God, and relying on Him to change us. It's like breathing. You exhale the sinful junk to God and inhale His cleansing and enabling Spirit. Paul instructs us to do this in Romans 12:1–2 (NIV): "Therefore, I urge you, brothers, in view of God's mercy, to offer your bodies as living sacrifices, holy and pleasing to God— this is your spiritual act of worship. Do not conform any longer to the pattern of this world, but be transformed by the renewing of your mind. Then you will be able to test and approve what God's will is—his good, pleasing and perfect will."

When you begin each day with this attitude, God's Spirit works in you and produces that fresh new feeling of freedom that makes life happy and fulfilling.

Start now by admitting you need self-control. Ask God to help you make a plan for your life every day and follow it. Cry out to God to help you see the areas of your life where you are vulnerable to temptation, and stay away from those temptations. And finally, pray that God will help you walk in the fullness of His Spirit day by day.

That is the true route to self-control as well as fulfillment in Christ.

WHERE
Do I Go from Here?

Applying the Principles of the Proverbs

Epilogue

Vernon Armitage has written a sound, practical book. As he has shown, the Bible's Book of Proverbs is full of wisdom for today's trials and tribulations. He's touched on everything from building your marriage to managing your money. It's amazing that even many generations before Christ people struggled with the same problems we face today.

If there is an overall principle to follow, though—one you should keep in your mind and heart at all times—it's that the fear of the Lord (reverence, respect, and love for Him) is the source and power of any form of wisdom you can find in the Bible. Begin with your relationship with God. That's the belt of truth that holds everything together. To try to follow these principles without a relationship with Him is not only foolish, it's impossible. God embedded in the truths of wisdom the need to draw on His power in order to live them out.

Our world is plunged into a war for the souls of people. That war rages around us every day. Victory comes only through trusting, living, and serving Jesus.

Before I ever became a Christian, I tried for many months to control my tongue. I had a serious cursing problem. I knew it was bad, sinful even, but I couldn't seem to shake it. The moment anything went wrong, a curse word escaped from my mouth like a wasp bent on stinging someone. My nickname around my fraternity house was "Gutter Gums" because of my incessant verbal garbage.

Later that year, I became an honest-to-goodness Christian. The transforming power I felt was incredible. I began obeying God's Word and following its principles like a child gamboling in the backyard with his father watching. Sheer joy accompanied my attempts to please God. In a short time, the Spirit pointed out my problem with cursing, and immediately I stopped. I found His power instant and solid. For years, under the Spirit's power, I've been able to control the problem.

God's power is available. If you look at the principles in this book and think, *It's impossible,* I would agree with you. In human terms, it is. But with God's help and power, anything is possible.

My counsel to you is to secure your relationship with Jesus before you ever try to live out this book. If you're not a Christian, become one. If you are a Christian who has slipped into sinful practices and carelessness, confess your sin, and get moving with Him. And if you are a consistent, determined follower of Christ, filled with His Spirit, show everyone you know that these principles can change one's life.

I'm glad you've read this far. I hope you have profited from the book. But above all, walk with Jesus. That's the bedrock truth that makes everything else in His kingdom work.

MARK LITTLETON

ENDNOTES

CHAPTER 1

1. David Hubbard, *Communicator's Commentary: Proverbs* (Nashville: W Publishing, 1989), 26.

2. Warren Wiersbe, *Be Skillful* (Colorado Springs: Chariot Victor, 1995), 11.

3. Roy Zuck, *Biblical Theology of the Old Testament* (Chicago: Moody Press, 1991), 232.

CHAPTER 2

1. Charles Swindoll, *Rise and Shine* (Grand Rapids, Mich.: Zondervan, 1989), 187.

2. Patrick Morley, *The Man in the Mirror* (Grand Rapids, Mich.: Zondervan, 2000), 154.

3. Morley, *The Man in the Mirror*, 156.

4. Naisbitt, *High Tech—High Touch* (London: Nicholas Brealey, 2001), 45.

CHAPTER 3

1. "TV Vs. Reality," *USA Today*, 6 July 1993, 1.

2. Richard Foster, *The Challenge of the Disciplined Life* (San Francisco: Harper, 1989), 91.

3. Ibid., 109.

4. Billy Graham, "AIDS, Sex and the Bible," *Decision*, October 1987, 1.

5. Jerry B. Jenkins, *Hedges: Loving Your Marriage Enough to Protect It* (Nashville: W Publishing, 1990), 75, 85, 93, 105, 113, 123.

CHAPTER 4

1. Zig Ziglar, *Top Performance* (New York: Berkley, 1991), 9.

2. Gary Inrig, *Quality Friendship* (Chicago: Moody Press, 1988), 40.

3. Paul Brand and Philip Yancey, *In His Image,* 25–29 [cited in Dennis Rainey, *Building Your Mate's Self-Esteem* (Nashville: Thomas Nelson, 1995), 22–23].

4. Alan McGinnis, *The Friendship Factor* (Minneapolis: Augsburg Fortress, 1979), 11.

5. Ibid., 159.

6. Ibid., 156.

7. *Draper's Book of Quotes for the Christian World CD, Bible Illustrator* software (Hiawatha, Iowa: Parson's Technology, 1990–1992).

CHAPTER 5

1. *USA Today,* 3 March 1999.

2. Lawrence Crabb, *Effective Biblical Counseling* (Grand Rapids, Mich.: Zondervan, 1977), 61.

3. Neil Clark Warren, *The Triumphant Marriage* (Colorado Springs: Focus on the Family, 1998), 8, 13.

4. H. Norman Wright, *Power of a Parent's Words* (Ventura, Calif.: Regal, 1991), 98.

5. Ibid., 96.

6. William Barclay, *The Letters to the Galatians and Ephesians* (Louisville, Ky.: Westminster John Knox, 2001), 211.

7. Neil Clark Warren, *Make Anger Your Ally* (Colorado Springs: Focus on the Family, 1990), 89.

8. Ibid., 18.

9. Warren, *The Triumphant Marriage,* 45.

10. David Augsburger, *Caring Enough to Confront* (Ventura, Calif.: Regal, 1981), 11.

CHAPTER 6

1. Warren Wiersbe, *Meet Your Conscience* (Wheaton, Ill.: Victor Books, 1983), 7.

2. Jay Kesler, *Parents and Children* (Colorado Springs: Chariot Victor, 1986), 450.

3. Kevin Leman Conference at Pleasant Valley Baptist Church, *Making Children Mind Without Losing Yours*.

CHAPTER 7

1. Foster, *The Challenge of the Disciplined Life*, 24.

2. Fred Smith, *You and Your Network* (Waco, Tex.: Word Books, 1984), 56.

3. Gene Getz, *Real Prosperity* (Chicago: Moody, 1990), 7.

4. Howard Hendricks, "Your Money and Your Life," *Discipleship Journal*, Issue 53, Sept/Oct 1989, 28.

5. Consumer Credit Counseling Services.

6. "Go Figure," *Christianity Today*, 7 October 1996, 21.

CHAPTER 8

1. Warren, *Make Anger Your Ally*, 121.

2. *Draper's Book of Quotes for the Christian World CD*.

CHAPTER 9

1. Michael P. Green, *Illustrations for Biblical Preaching* (Grand Rapids, Mich.: Baker, 1990), 20.

2. Warren, *Make Anger Your Ally*, 77.

3. Les Carter, *Good 'n Angry* (Grand Rapids, Mich.: Baker, 1983), 28.

4. Warren, *Make Anger Your Ally*, 87.

CHAPTER 10

1. John Casey, "Real Giving," *Preaching Today,* tape no. 156.

2. James Dobson, *When God Doesn't Make Sense* (Wheaton, Ill.: Tyndale, 2001), 77.

3. Ibid., 17.

4. Bill Hybels, *Making Life Work, Trust God* (South Barriington, Ill.: Seeds Tape Ministry, 1998), audiotape #1221.